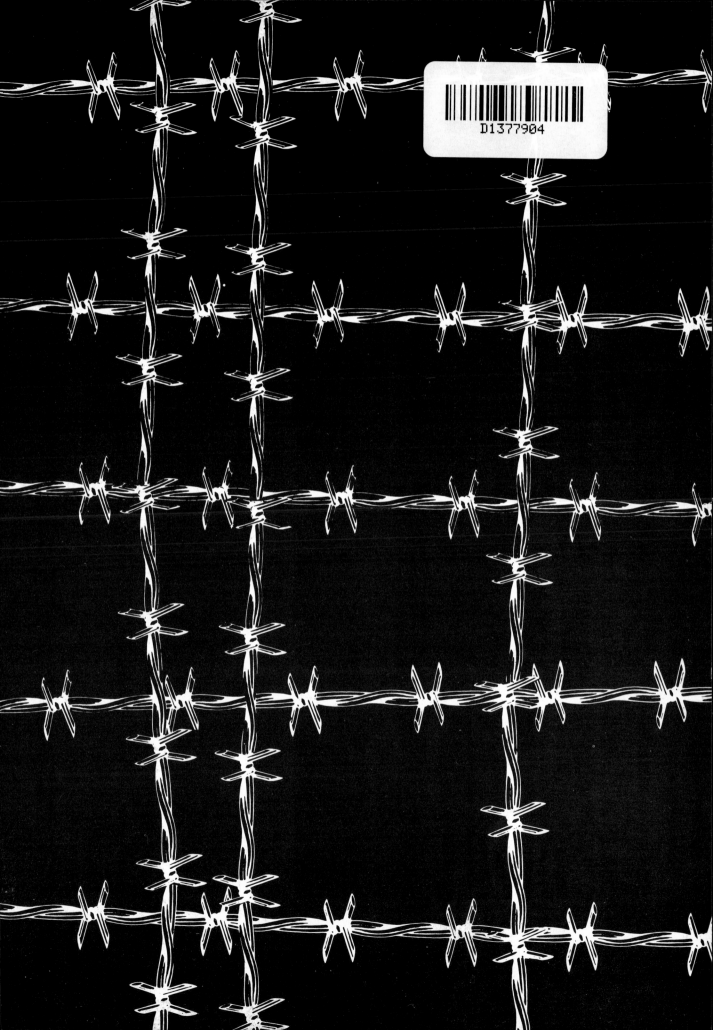

ESCAPE
FROM THE
SWASTIKA

Marshall Cavendish

PICTURES SUPPLIED BY:

Auckland Star 23.
BBC Publications 31.
Jack Best 32.
Michael Booker 29, 31, 32, 34.
Michael Booker/Red Cross 35.
British Lion Films 90/91.
Mme A. Brusselmans 102, 103, 105, 107, 108, 109, 110, 111.
Collins Ltd. 70.
Dr. Reinhold Eggers 8, 10, 11, 12, 13, 14, 16, 17, 20.
Hodder & Stoughton 15.
Imperial War Museum 37, 40, 41, 46, 47, 52, 53, 56, 88, 92, 93, 94, 95, 112, 114, 114/115.
Ley Kenyon 4/5, 36, 38/39, 41, 43, 44/45, 48/49, 51, 54/55.
Pan Books/Universal Tandem 24, 28.
Richard Pape 72, 76, 77, 81, 86, 87.
Photo Research International 57, 58/59, 63, 64.
Popperfoto 27, 29, 89, 96, 97, 98/99, 99, 101, 113.
Red Cross Archives 7, 9, 74/75, 78, 79, 80, 82, 83, 84/85, 116/117, 118, 119, 120.
Pat Reid 34.
Tanjug Fotos 68/69, 71.
U.S. Air Force 61, 66/67.
John Watton 19.

Our thanks to Squadron Leader Gilbert of the RAF Escaping Society for helping us to trace some of the individuals mentioned in this book, and to Mrs Fawcett, Librarian of the Red Cross Archives, for her help.

The précis of the book *The Wooden Horse* by Eric Williams, published in the UK by William Collins Sons & Co. Ltd., is printed by permission of the author.

Material based on the books *Boldness Be My Friend* and *Sequel to Boldness* by Richard Pape is printed by permission of the author.

Published by Marshall Cavendish Books Limited,
58 Old Compton Street, London W1V 5PA

© Marshall Cavendish Limited 1975, 1983

This volume first printed 1975

ISBN 0 85685 108 6

THIS VOLUME IS NOT TO BE SOLD IN AUSTRALIA, NEW ZEALAND OR NORTH AMERICA.

Printed in Italy by New Interlitho S.p.A. - Milan

INTRODUCTION

Bravery and ingenuity — against the efficency of the Wehrmact, the frightening interrogation of the Gestapo, and the dogged persistence of p.o.w. camp guards — were the twin qualities that took men through barbed wire and claustrophobic tunnels into some of the most hair raising situations of World War II as they crossed hundreds of miles of enemy held territory.

In *Escape from the Swastika* you will share the drawn-out tension of some of the most exciting escapes of the entire war: from Colditz, a blitz-out straight through the wire, from under the noses of the Gestapo in Brussels, the biggest escape of all and many more.

Photographs of the people and places involved, illustrations — many in full colour — of escape gear and maps and diagrams to show escape routes and techniques put you right in the picture.

And to add that final touch of authenticity many details have been checked by the only people who know what it was really like . . . the people who actually took part in the escapes. Ley Kenyon's pictures of 'The Tunnellers' were drawn at the time in Stalag Luft III — and recovered after the war. And from the other side, extracts from the diary of Dr Reinhold Eggers, Security Officer at Colditz, tell the German reaction.

Escape from Swastika gives you the thrills — and the background.

CONTENTS

N

SWEDEN

STOCKHOLM

GOTEBORG
The Wooden
Horse

BRITAIN

AMSTERDAM

STETTIN• The Tunnellers

POLAND

BERLIN• The Wirecutters

The Wirecutters
The Wooden Horse
The Tunnellers

GERMANY

Stalag Luft III

Rendezvous 127
BRUSSELS

BRESLAU

Stalag VIIIB Escape from
Hell Camp

Dulag Luft
Escape from
Hell Camp

COLDITZ
Oflag IVC

CRACOW

PARIS•

CZECH

AUSTRIA

HUNGARY

FRANCE

SWITZ

ITALY

YUGOSLAVIA

BELGRADE•

Survival in Yugoslavia
PODGORICA (TITOGRAD)

Escape from
Salonika Dulag 183
SALONIKA

ATH

GREECE

ATHEN

COLDITZ

In the brooding mediaeval castle of Colditz, the most seasoned escapers of the Second World War tried everything—from long, twisting tunnels to a glider that was to fly across the wall. But Captain 'Lulu' Lawton and five accomplices took the easy way—marching out through the main gate.

Colditz is the most famous of World War II prisoner-of-war camps, probably because of the exploits of its inmates — and probably because, in contrast to the dreary ugliness of other POW camps, it is a stark and forbidding mediaeval castle, the first sight of which is enough to make the bravest quail.

Colditz Castle, built in the eleventh century on a cliff-top from which it dominates the romantic-looking little town of the same name on the banks of the River Mulde in Upper Saxony, has a history of bloodshed and oppression, and had been a prison since 1800, a lunatic asylum since 1828. The first sight of its gaunt, majestic shape sent an icicle into the heart of many an Allied prisoner seeing it for the first time.

Previous page and below Colditz Castle was supposed to be impregnable. Yet the 200 officer prisoners burrowed and schemed and notched up literally hundreds of escape attempts ranging from complicated tunnels and even a glider to fly over the walls to the simple plan of Captain 'Lulu' Lawton—he walked out.
Opposite Volley ball in the prisoners' courtyard might cover preparations for escape.

From as early in the war as 1940, they came to Colditz singly, or in small groups—Poles, Frenchmen, Britons, Canadians, Australians, New Zealanders, South Africans, Dutchmen, and later, Americans—all of whom had been classified as 'undesirable' by the German authorities, some because of their politics, some for their hatred of everything German, but mainly because they had made escape attempts from other camps.

The prisoner-strength of the camp was approximately 200, and to guard them was a German staff consisting of a Commandant and about a dozen other officers and half a dozen NCOs, plus a guard company of about 150 men with their own Commanding Officer and NCOs.

The prisoners of Colditz had one thing in common—their whole-hearted desire to escape. The castle's forbidding appearance and reputation for impregnability only served to sharpen their desire to outwit the German authorities—even though the closest frontier not directly under the Nazi heel was a daunting 400 hostile miles away.

Swift and simple

By September 1942, many escape methods had been tried, but few had been successful. Literally dozens of tunnels had been built, but nearly all of these had been discovered before they could be used. What the prisoners were searching for—and were constantly thinking about in almost every waking moment, almost to the point of obsession—was a method of getting out that was swift, simple and audacious.

Captain 'Lulu' Lawton, of the Duke of Wellington Regiment, hit upon such a method.

It had evolved over a period of several weeks, beginning—as most escape plans did—with a wild flash of inspiration, when he saw an opportunity that no one else had noticed.

For months he had been watching the comings and goings of visitors to and from the Castle. His mind had registered the fact that on two or three mornings a week, a small party of Polish POWs who were billeted in the town was marched up to the Castle under the command of a German NCO and accompanied by a German private.

He made a record of the times, and found that the arrival of the 'fatigue' party could be at any hour of the day. But mostly it occurred in the morning, sometimes as early as 0700 hours. And the routine was always the same. The Polish prisoners, carrying parcels or boxes of clothing or equipment would be marched into the store-room. They would stay there for about half an hour, then march out again, generally carrying large wooden boxes, two men per box.

It was common knowledge that the sentries on the gate were changed at 0700. Therefore, Lawton reasoned, the time for the escape attempt must be shortly after the day-shift had taken over.

Lawton could easily visualize four prisoners, wearing Polish uniforms and carrying two wooden boxes between them, and escorted by two prisoners—one dressed as a senior German NCO and the other as a German private—walking through the gate one morning and escaping to freedom.

After studying a plan of the castle which the Escape Committee provided for him, he decided that his escape party must emerge from some-where in the vicinity of the storeroom, and the RSM's office seemed to offer the likeliest pros-

Left Stooge Wardle was one of the five who escaped with 'Lulu' Lawton.
Below The Dutchman Van Doorninck (known as Rip Van Winkle) picked the locks that made escape possible and acted as the German NCO. He and **right** Bill Fowler got clean away.
Far right Stabsfeldwebel Gephard was chief orderly. It was through the floor of his office that the escapers made a hole into the storeroom.
Dr Rheingold Eggers, Security Officer at Colditz writes: The p.o.w.s called him Mussolini. I now know for sure that he was bribed by the p.o.w.s but I think that in 1942 he was still loyal to his superiors. In my Colditz diary I said—Now the most extravagant happening: Priem found the hole by which the escapers reached freedom (this was after roll-calls had established six were missing). The hole, already walled up again, was under the very table of Stabsfeldwebel Gephard in his office! Openly the 'sick' had broken in, burrowed through the floor and reached an outside annex used as a storeroom. Soon after seven a.m. the door to the storeroom opened and an officer came out. Hè was followed by four Polish orderlies carrying two wooden cases and a corporal who closed and locked the door. Sentry No. 6 saw all this in full daylight and did—nothing.

pect. The first idea that occurred to him was, of course, tunnelling, but he discarded it. Tunnelling was for rabbits—people without imagination. The time it took to build a tunnel was the method's greatest hazard. Anyway, there were already far too many tunnels crisscrossing beneath the castle's foundations, and the Jerries were constantly searching for them.

He decided that the best way of reaching the RSM's office was via the sick-ward—not by tunnelling, but by the simple device of opening the doors that stood in the way.

Lock picking

His first step was to approach Captain Van Doorninck, a red-headed Dutchman who was known throughout the compound as an expert in repairing instruments and watches. As Van Doorninck often repaired watches for the Germans, he had been able to assemble a kit of tools that would be ideal for solving the problems of the locks.

Van Doorninck heard the Englishman's plan in silence, then nodded. He had once been a lock-smith. What he needed to know was what kind of locks he would be dealing with.

Lawton pleaded sickness and spent two days and a night in the sick-ward, during which time he was able to examine the locks, not only leading from the sick-ward to the corridor, but from the corridor to the RSM's office. He described the cross-shaped keyholes to Van Doorninck. Like a Yale lock, but with four arms.

The Dutchman nodded. The cruciform. He made a quick sketch of the key-hole, and Lawton agreed that he had identified it correctly. Van Doorninck described the lock's innards. There were tiny pistons inside cylinders, about six to nine of them, and when you inserted the key, these pistons moved a different distance—to an accuracy of one thousandth of an inch. He could make such a key.

His first step was to make a special micrometer gauge. Then he made a key, using the gauge to check the lifting faces of the key as he filed them. He had to visit a friend in the sick-ward to physically check his first key in the lock, and within a few days he had made it.

At night he let himself into the corridor and tackled the door to the RSM's office. There were, in fact, two locks on this door—one a padlock—

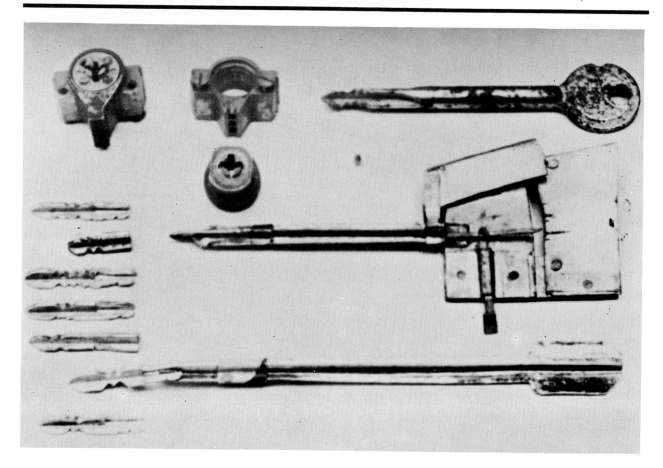

Captain Van Doorninck constructed these devices to pick his way through the intricacies of the Zeiss cruciform lock on the Stabsfeldwebel's door. A jemmy saw to the simpler locks.

but they presented no difficulty to Van Doorninck. And within another few days, this first essential phase of the operation was complete.

Van Doorninck had other attributes. He looked like a German. And he spoke German fluently. He was obviously the ideal choice for the senior German NCO who would march the 'fatigue' party out of the compound.

They brought in another Dutchman, Lieutenant Donkers, to play the role of the German private.

The 'Polish' members of the party were to be Lawton himself, Flight Lieutenant Bill Fowler, RAF, 'Stooge' Wardle, a submarine type, and one other, Beets.

By now the escape plan had been approved by the Escape Committee, which gave it practical support in various ways. Captain Pat Reid worked closely with Lawton at all stages, and Dick Howe

was put in charge. Ken Lockwood was seconded as an active accomplice who would work inside the sick-ward and manipulate the keys.

Reconnaisance

The night came for them to take a look inside the office of Oberstabsfeldwebel Gephard—the RSM.

Lockwood, who had gone sick with stomach pains, was given the keys. Reid and Howe visited him after evening *appell* and hid under the beds until after lights out. Then Lockwood opened the doors for Reid and Howe to go through into the RSM's office. He locked them in and returned to his bed. The two men, with a shaded flashlight, began their examination of the small, narrow, rectangular office.

At the end farthest from the door, there was a barred window in a narrow alcove, set high in the wall. It would be difficult to scramble out of in broad daylight without being seen.

The walls of the office were lined with shelves which were crammed with books, files, batteries, hurricane lamps, boxes of nails and screws, coils of wire, and so on.

Beneath Gephard's desk, Reid made an examination of the wooden floor, then measured the distance to the wall that connected it with the storeroom, which was on a lower level.

Lockwood came back 30 minutes later and let them out, then relocked the office. They stole back to the sick-ward and hid under the beds until after the medical orderly had made his early morning rounds. Then they went back to their quarters.

After *appell* they met Lawton and Van Doorninck.

They didn't like the window, Reid told them. As an exit it was very dangerous. They should forget it as a possible escape exit. The alternative, he said, and Howe agreed with him, was the storeroom which adjoined the office though on a much lower level. It could be reached by making a short tunnel from beneath the RSM's desk and breaking through the dividing wall, which he estimated was about 18 inches thick.

Lawton and Van Doorninck enthusiastically accepted this suggestion, which had obvious advantages and which eliminated the weakest point in the plan—the escape from the window. From the storeroom, the party would be able to march out in full view on to the sentry path as did the *real* parties.

The lock on the storeroom door? Was it another cruciform? Or an ordinary lever lock as on most exterior doors of the castle? They would have to find out.

For the next few days a continuous watch was kept on the entrance to the storeroom. Unfortunately the door itself could not be seen from the only vantage point available to them, but anyone approaching the entrance could be seen as he neared the door.

One morning, an NCO storeman came into view. As he approached the door he took out a

key chain and selected a key. Then he stepped out of sight to open the door. The watcher had seen the key and identified it. It was one of the type used to open an ordinary lever lock. It would present no problem to Van Doorninck using a simple jemmy.

Tunnelling through

So now the work could commence on the tunnel. That evening, with the help of Lockwood, Reid and Derek Gill, of the Royal Norfolks, spent several hours locked inside the RSM's office.

First of all, they moved the desk. Then, working as quietly as possible, they prised up the floorboards and scooped away the under-floor rubble to make a short tunnel leading to the wall of the storeroom. Taking turns in working inside the tunnel, they reached the wall of the storeroom.

They found that the mortar between the stones was old, and with the sharp chisels and spikes they used they were easily loosened. One by one, the stones came out, to reveal that they faced on to a plaster wall.

At this point, they put the stones back in place and backed out of the tunnel. They spread blankets inside the tunnel to muffle the hollowness, then carefully replaced the floorboards, sealed the cracks with a dust-coloured paste, and swept up. Then they put the desk back exactly in

The escapers built this wooden sewing machine so they could make authentic-looking uniforms for the 'German' soldiers and 'Polish' orderlies. Sentries and guards were taken in.

its original place and waited for Lockwood to come and let them through to the sick-ward.

On the following night they went back and enlarged the hole and made everything ready for the escape. Everything went according to plan, and in the morning they strolled out of the sick-ward on to the parade ground for early morning *appell.*

In the meantime, many people in the compound had been working to back up the escapers by providing such essentials as identity papers, the German and Polish uniforms, and civilian clothes. Also, two large boxes were made up, then dismantled into sections which were smuggled into the sick-ward and hidden under the beds, as were all the other bulky items needed for the escape.

Lawton had been keeping a continuous watch on the entrance, waiting for a genuine 'fatigue' party to enter the castle, then leave. When it happened, he made plans to make the escape

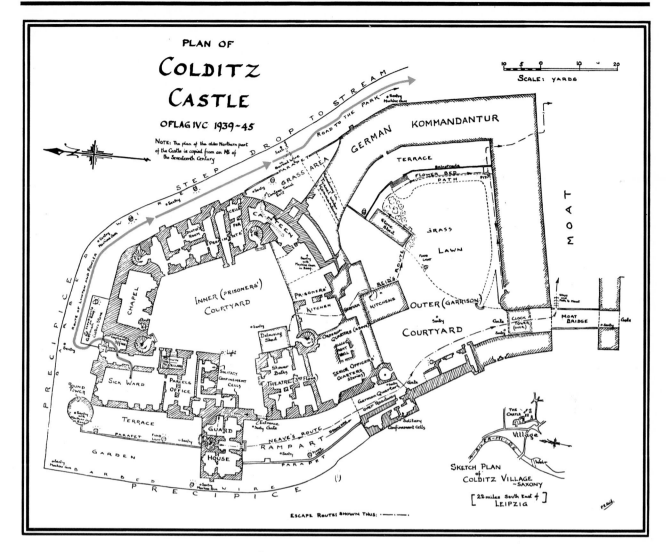

PLAN OF
COLDITZ
CASTLE
OFLAG IVC 1939~45

NOTE: The plan of the older Northern part of the Castle is copied from an MS of the Seventeenth Century

SCALE: YARDS

SKETCH PLAN of COLDITZ VILLAGE ~SAXONY

[22 miles South East of LEIPZIG]

ESCAPE ROUTES SHOWN THUS: ·——·

Left *The marked door, in the north-west corner of the prisoners' yard at Colditz, led to the sick-room and Stabsfeldwebel Gephard's room. From here* **below** *the escapers emerged into the storeroom, the additional building outside the chapel, opened the door and walked down the staircase to the pathway round the castle used by the sentries.*
Above *The escapers' route took them alongside the castle and past several sentries. Dr Reinhold Eggers writes: They met sentry No. 5. He saw the officer's uniform, stood to attention and most probably reported to the 'officer'—'Nothing new in this area!'*

attempt on the following day, feeling that this now lessened the chances of running into a real party.

That evening after *appell*, eight men made

their way at intervals into the sick-ward and hid themselves under the beds.

'Lights out' came just after dark, and silence fell over the castle.

Just after 2130 hours, Lockwood got out of bed and went to the latrine to relieve himself and assess the lie of the land. Everything was normal and quiet.

He unlocked the door leading into the corridor and went through. The eight men crawled from their hiding places and stole like ghosts along the dark corridor, carrying the bundles of clothing and pieces of the dismantled boxes.

Lockwood unlocked the two locks of the door to the RSM's office, led the men through, re-locked the door and went back to bed in the sick-ward.

The eight men sat on the floor, huddled together in the tomb-like blackness to wait.

This door, Herr Hauptmann ?

The time passed. 2200 hours. 2300. Midnight.
They heard footsteps in the corridor. Then a line of light showed beneath the door, and the knob turned.

The Germans themselves re-enacted the escape— after they worked out how it had been done—and took photographs of themselves doing so.
***Above** The 'escapers' marched along the path beside the castle taken by Lawton's group and then **right** out through the Green Gate that marked the end of the prison compound.*

A voice said in German:
'*This* door, Herr Hauptmann?'
They held their breath.
'Yes, please. Open it,' Hauptmann Priem snapped.
'But it is the office of Stabsfeldwebel Gephard, Herr Hauptmann—'
'I said "Open!"'
'Yes, Herr Hauptmann.'
There was a metallic rattle of keys. It seemed to go on interminably. The men had resigned themselves to the fact that the game was up, and braced themselves for what would follow.
Hauptmann Priem said brusquely: 'Never mind! Herr Gephard has so many locks. I forgot. Come!'
'Yes, Herr Hauptmann.'
Footsteps retreated along the corridor. Then there was silence.
'Phew!' someone breathed.
They waited until 0300 hours.
Then Reid, who was on the dog-watch, began to work alone. He removed the floorboards under the RSM's desk and stacked them carefully out of the way. Then, taking a torch, he crawled down the tunnel. He carefully removed the stones from the face and put each one behind him. Only a thin wall of plaster-board remained between him and the storeroom.
He took out a sharp pointed knife and cut a small hole in the centre of the face, slicing the

plaster at an angle so that the pieces fell inside the tunnel. But some pieces inevitably fell into the storeroom, making a sharp clatter.

He stopped and listened for a while, then began to work more carefully. Soon he was able to put his hand through the hole and break off pieces of plaster and pull them inwards. At last he had cleared the hole at the end of the tunnel; it was ready for the first man to go through to the storeroom.

He crawled backwards up the tunnel, emerged from beneath the desk and told the men it was time to move.

Dutch talent pays off

Van Doorninck went down first, going backwards. When he reached the hole in the wall he lay face down and lowered himself into the pitch-black storeroom, feet first. His feet encountered a shelf. He eased his weight on to it with one foot, then felt further down with the other. He found another shelf. He went down further, hoping that the shelving was securely anchored to the wall. He let go of the stonework at the bottom of the hole and climbed down, using the shelves as rungs of a ladder. Presently his feet stood on an asphalt floor.

He switched on his torch and made a quick examination of the storeroom. It was roomy, but crammed with packing cases filled with equipment. He crossed to the outer door, switched off his torch and waited, his ear pressed against the upper panel.

He stayed like that for a time, listening for any sound, but none reached him.

He took out the small jemmy which he had fashioned expressly for this moment. He found the key-hole in the darkness, inserted the jemmy, turned it gently. The bolt clicked back beautifully. He locked it again and pocketed the jemmy.

Lawton was already waiting at the mouth of the tunnel, and Van Doorninck gave him the good news. Lawton climbed down. The four other officers followed him. Then Reid and Gill passed down the sections of the wooden boxes, the bundles of clothing, and finally some water bottles and a bucket of plaster.

When everything was down, Reid stayed in the tunnel and began to replace the stones to close up the hole, Van Doorninck, standing on the shelves, applied a thick coating of plaster to the face of the stones as they were put in place and secured with mortar.

Finally, there was just a small rectangular hole to be filled in—room for the last stone to go into place. Reid and Van Doorninck had their last look at each other and grinned. They had a few words and checked their watches. It was 0547.

Reid whispered: 'Good luck!'

He pushed the last stone into the hole and closed it, then secured it with mortar. On the other side, Van Doorninck finished plastering the face, then climbed down with the bucket and the water bottles.

Reid and Gill replaced the floorboards, filled the cracks with mud-paste, put the RSM's desk back in place, and swept up.

Lockwood came and opened the door at 0600 hours, let them through, then locked up. They went into the sick-ward and hid under the beds until the medical orderly had done his rounds.

At 0710, the six escapers, disguised as a German NCO, a German Private, and four Polish orderlies, came out of the storeroom on the north side of the castle. The 'Poles' were carrying the two wooden boxes. Van Doorninck led the party along the path to the barbed-wire gate.

The German sentries saluted smartly as the squad passed them, and at the gate, the sentry in charge unlocked it. The party passed through.

They were out of the prison compound. They proceeded downhill along the roadway to the large arched doorway in the massive wall that surrounded the castle grounds. A German NCO stood framed in the archway, watching their approach.

'Are you going to Zschadrass?' he asked.

'Yes,' Van Doorninck answered.

'Then I will open the door for you,' the NCO said obligingly.

On the morning after the escape the antics of the remaining prisoners so confused the guards that it took four roll-calls, the last at 2.30 p.m., to establish that three British and three Dutch prisoners were missing.

The German dog squad discovered the uniforms abandoned by the escapers—a woman from the town reported them too—but could not follow

He turned and opened the door, pulled it wide open to allow them to pass. They marched into the open countryside, heading for the village.

It remained for the prisoners back in camp to delay discovery of the escape for as long as possible and thus to buy time for the escapers, who had quickly changed into civilian clothes, hidden the two boxes full of discarded uniforms, and split up into parties of two to make for the Swiss border.

At 0830, the morning *appell* parade mustered in a state of controlled confusion. A lot of the prisoners seemed overcome by sickness this morning, and had remained in their bunks, holding their stomachs and groaning, or making feverish sorties to the lavatories. The parade was such a chaos that the Commandant dismissed it and ordered a second *appell* for 0915.

But at 0900, the Commandant's office received a phone message from the military police in the township. A woman had found two boxes containing Polish and German uniforms near the Tiergarten above the park.

The Commandant put the phone down and muttered:

'The *sauhaufen* (pig-mob)! That's why there's been so much trouble this morning!'

He ordered reinforcements to attend the parade, and they soon found that six officers were missing. Immediately, steps were taken to hunt them down.

Unfortunately, the man who master-minded the brilliant and audacious escape—Captain Lawton—and his running mate were caught later in the day. And on the following day, so were Wardle and Donkers.

But Van Doorninck and Bill Fowler got clean away from the area and reached Switzerland six days later.

ESCAPE FROM SALONIKA

In an infamous prison camp in the north of Greece, New Zealander 'Sandy' Thomas sketched out his one-way ticket to freedom—a few hundred yards through the sick-bay, over a road and out through the wire. Easy—except for the criss-crossing searchlights and the dozens of sentries.

Prison camps in Greece were infamous—and Salonika was the worst of all. Conditions were bad and the guards treated the prisoners as less than animals. The compound Lieutenant 'Sandy' Thomas found himself in contained seven barracks huts like this one and was guarded by four sentry posts with searchlights and machine-guns.

On May 24, 1941, units of the 23rd New Zealand Battalion were captured on Crete during the German airborne invasion. Among the prisoners was Second Lieutenant W. B. Thomas, who had received a bayonet through the left thigh and multiple grenade wounds during the bloody Battle of Galatas. After a day and night of morphia-induced twilight, Thomas found himself flying north in a German transport plane, and was taken to the captured 5th Australian General Hospital in Athens.

May, June, July and early August were marked off on Thomas's calendar, during which his painful leg wound partially recovered, and his thoughts turned to escape. He made several abortive attempts, including once by pretending to die—he got to the point of being carried out of the ward in a coffin, but the whole ruse amused him so much that he burst into uncontrolled laughter and gave the game away. After failing in a final audacious escape attempt he was transferred to the specially guarded camp at Salonika, as a stage on the way to Germany.

Salonika Prison Camp was infamous in every way. Many shocking atrocities had been committed there by guards who had come from Hitler's Youth Movement.

When Lieutenant 'Sandy' Thomas arrived there in October 1941, the camp was still shattered by the aftermath of a horrendous case—a German sentry had thrown a grenade into a latrine full of prisoners causing many casualties. His excuse was that they were whispering together in a suspicious manner.

On his arrival at the camp, he was allotted a bed in a room shared by a regular officer, Major Richard Burnett, who had been CO of his unit on Crete. It wasn't very long before Thomas's enthusiasm had infected Burnett, and together they planned to escape.

Their subsection of the camp comprised a compound about 300 hundred yards long and 200 wide. It contained seven long barracks blocks, a cook-house and a large new building partly occupied by the hospital ward. The camp was guarded at the southern end by two 20-foot towers, each with a movable searchlight and a machine-gun, and manned by two sentries. At the northern end, on the roof of a small shed, there was another manned sentry-post equipped with a searchlight.

Plans for escape

For several days and nights, Thomas and Burnett watched the routine of the camp and the movement of the sentries. After making diagrams, they came to the conclusion that the southern and western sides of the compound, which joined other subsections, were too dangerous to contemplate. So, too, was the northern (rear) side with its roof-based searchlight. This left only the east side, which was enclosed by a barbed-wire barricade broken by two buildings— the cookhouse, which was a stone's throw from one of the southern sentry towers, and the new three-storey building, the ground floor of which was occupied by the hospital ward.

This latter building seemed to offer some slender chance of escape. The windows facing east—away from the camp—were heavily barred and covered with barbed wire. They were in full view of the searchlights at both ends of the compound which constantly played on the road outside the barricade. But the building was easily accessible; one had only to visit an inmate in the hospital, then sneak upstairs to the vacant first floor, from which there was an outside staircase leading down to the road.

One evening after *appell* or roll call, the two men went into the building and made a full examination of the first floor. They looked at the angle of the searchlights and found that the one on one of the southern towers had an unobstructed view of the rear of the building. But the position of the one on the shed roof

'Sandy' Thomas was determined to escape from Salonika before he could be transferred to a more secure prison camp in Germany.

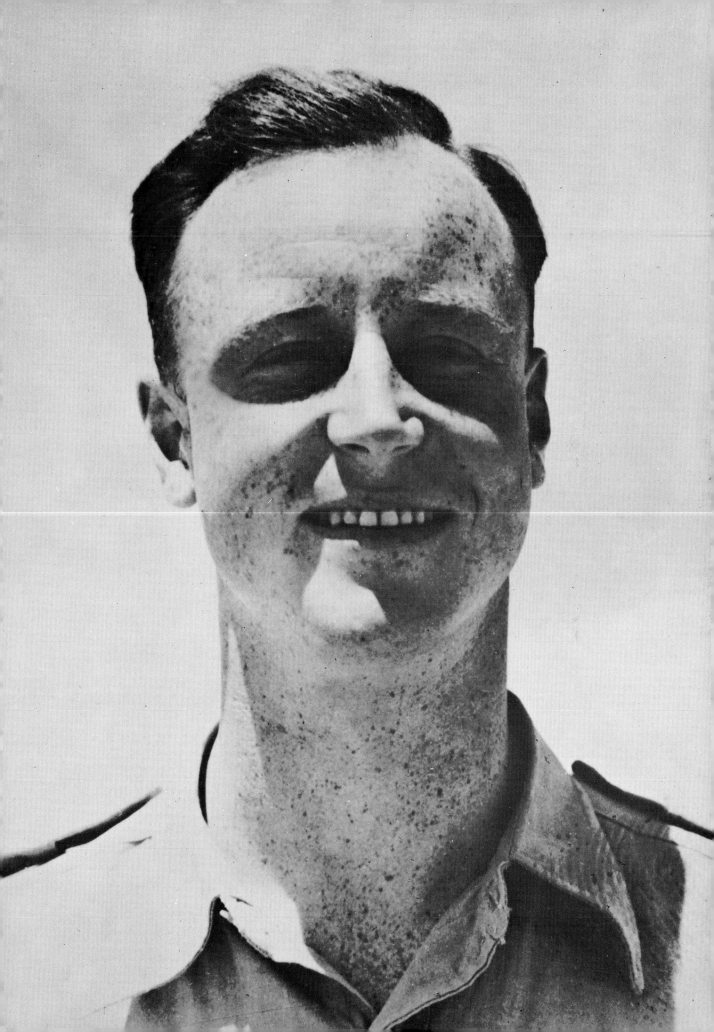

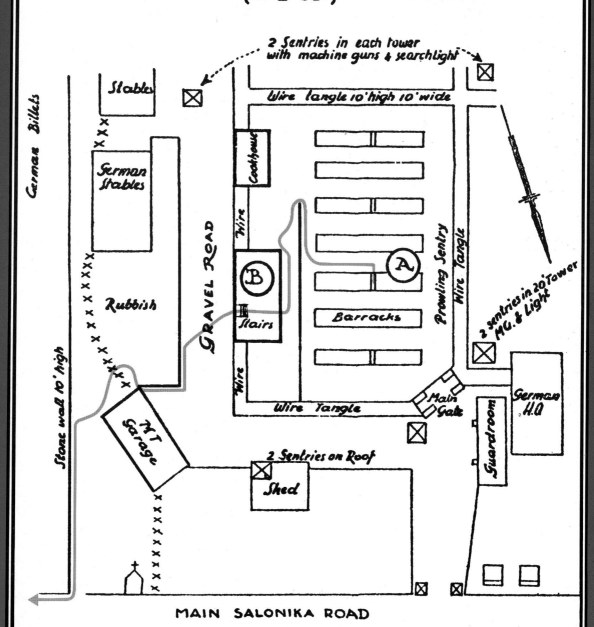

SALONIKA CAMP
(SUB SEC)

A   The barrack in which I shared a room with Burnett

B   The three-storeyed building for medical orderlies

—·—·—The route I took on the night of my escape

Freedom was only a few hundred yards away but Thomas risked death at every step as the search-lights—and machine-guns—swept the compound.

prevented it from lighting up the rear wall or the door which they contemplated using. The search-lights were on swivels, and they swung their beams across the compound every few seconds to cover the perimeter. The highest priority, of course, was given to covering the road. But with both searchlight crews independently swinging their beams over the compound, the road was periodically left in darkness for a few seconds at a time.

Now they examined the doorway. The steel door-frame was set into the stone wall. The door itself was steel, with steel and wooden bars bolted across it. Outside, steps ran down in two short flights, turning at a small landing. The whole structure was covered with a tangle of barbed wire.

Tools for the job

The would-be escapers began to gather tools for the job. Thomas bought a pair of pliers from a Greek electrician working in the barracks. Burnett made some sturdy crowbars. And from one of the medical orderlies, they obtained a strong pair of plastic cutters.

One day after the evening check, they got their tools and hid them under their clothes and strolled into the hospital ward. After visiting a friend, they stole upstairs and hid behind some crates until lights out. Then they went to work.

Quietly and unhurriedly, they prised out the screws, bolts and nails holding the bars. By 0400 they had removed all the wooden bars and six of the steel ones. They nailed them back into place, tidied up, hid their tools, and stole back to their barracks.

On the following night they came back again. They managed to remove two more steel bars and loosen a third. But the roving sentries outside on the road seemed more active than usual, and they had to stop work several times and wait in the darkness for long periods.

On the third night they were able to remove the last of the steel bars. Then they tried the door. Incredibly, it was unlocked, and they were able to open it and pull it inwards—but only three inches. It was securely held by the barbed wire barricade outside. Once again, they put everything back into place and stole back to their barracks.

The two men received a shock when only a minute or two after they had climbed into their bunks, the door of the hut burst open and three German guards came in. They flashed torches in every face and pulled back the blankets of every bunk, paying particular attention to Thomas. Then, finally satisfied that all was normal, they marched from the hut and banged the door.

They're on to us

On the following morning, Thomas received a bombshell. After a sleepness night, Burnett had decided against the escape.

'They're on to us', he told Thomas.

Thomas went into the building to see if their work had been disturbed. He found the bars intact, their tools where they had left them. He went back to the barracks and told Burnett.

The Major shook his head. 'It's a trap. I feel it in my bones.'

Reluctantly, Thomas decided to go it alone, and immediately. He had managed to accumulate 8,000 drachmae, and Burnett gave him all his savings and cooked him a farewell dinner.

At last, after curfew, he was ready to leave. He put on a civilian overcoat and a beret and stood by the door, ready to let himself out into the compound. The searchlights seemed to rove across the camp incessantly, restlessly. A roving patrol of two guards paused for a time outside his hut and conversed in low tones. They finally moved off. Thomas let himself out. It took him almost an hour to cross the 200 yards to the hospital building.

When he got there, one of his friends, a patient, was horrified at seeing him out after curfew, knowing that the guards would shoot on sight. He tried to persuade the New Zealander to give up his escape attempt. Thomas shook his head and stole up the stairs to the dark first floor. The patient feverishly kept watch from a window of the ward.

Everything was quiet and normal. He went to the escape door. It was just as he had left it. He quietly removed all the nails holding bars. Then he opened the door and pulled it inwards. It moved three inches, stopped, held securely by the barbed-wire barricade outside. With the cutters, he cut away all the strands crossing the slit of the open door, and one by one they curled back.

He heard a sudden *slap* of leather from below. His friend slapping his slipper on the stairs to warn him that a sentry was coming. He quickly pushed the door shut and stood like a statue in the semi-darkness.

A heavy pair of boots crunched stolidly on the gravel road below. His heart was in his mouth, for he felt certain that the loose ends of the barbed-wire coiling back from the door must be spotted by the sentry. He waited for the footsteps to slow down, to stop, but they didn't. They went on past with the same unhurried rhythm, and faded.

For a long time, Thomas stood still, listening. Then his friend below began to whistle a tune from the opera *Rigoletto*. All was clear again.

He pulled the door inwards. It moved easily. He swung it wide enough for him to look through, to get a clear view of the road. The angle of the doorway was so acute that provided he did not put head right through, he would not be seen from either tower.

Between them, the two searchlights covering this side of the compound seemed to criss-cross almost continuously. The one on the southern tower seemed more than usually vigilant, the bright disc of its beam moving constantly up and down the road.

Presently a team of horses came clattering up the road, with the grinding of steel-rimmed wheels. The searchlights caught them in their beams, moved along with them, then the southern searchlight jerked ahead of them to the stables. It offered an opportunity. Thomas braced himself in the doorway.

Slap!

The slipper hit the stairs. He closed the door and waited.

The 2200 hours relief guard came marching up the road. Crunch crunch crunch crunch . . . the corporal snapped an order . . . crunch crunch crunch crunch . . . the footsteps faded away.

Christ! Thomas thought, I could have run right into them!

He waited now until the guard was changed, and for the off-duty sentries to march back to the guard-room. Then silence. Then his friend below, whistling *Rigoletto*.

The new guard began vigilantly, and the searchlights from both ends of the compound swept the road, quickly at first, then more slowly, steadily, settling down to the long night's vigil.

Thomas began to count the lengths of the breaks of darkness that the routine produced.

'One . . . two . . . three . . . one . . . two . . . three . . .'

A long period of light.

'One . . . two . . . three . . . four . . .'

It was impossible to out-guess them, with two independent searchlights playing over the area. It was a matter of luck.

Time after time he braced himself, ready to run. Each time, a searchlight's disc of light darted to the road below him. One moment he was chilled with fear at the nearness of his escape; then he kicked himself for not going when he should have.

He went.

He moved down the steps swiftly and smoothly, not running. He swung around on the landing, went down the other short flight to the ground, then darted across the road and flung himself flat at the foot of the low wall.

Searchlights and wire

One of the lights swept back—the one from the shed roof. Then the light from the tower joined it. They criss-crossed over the wall, the road, while Thomas lay face down, blinded by the glare, his body tingling with fear, his spine bristling, expecting at any instant a savage hail of bullets.

It was only a matter of seconds, but the wait

here seemed to go on forever. He could hear German sentries talking up in the southern tower, quietly, with no hint of excitement or alarm.

The lights were gone. He was in blackness. He rose quickly, sprang in beside the MT garage and dropped behind a large oil drum.

One of the lights swept back, tentative, searching. It went away again.

He swung himself over the low wall and lay still. For the time being he was safe from the searchlights and hidden in the deep shadow of the wall.

He moved along it several yards, then waited for the darkness before moving away. He crawled along through scattered piles of rubbish and clumps of shrub. When the light came back, he stayed still, his shape mingling with the broken pattern of shadows thrown by the rubbish. The darkness came and he moved on, further away from the compound.

Ten yards. 200. 300. To the outer ring of double-apron barbed wire. He produced his cutters and snipped his way through the barricade.

He headed outward from the camp and run into something he hadn't bargained for—a ten-foot high fence of wire mesh, too strong for his cutters. He bent double and ran along beside it, searching for a way out, aware that he was liable to be spotted at any instant by roving pickets outside the perimeter.

He found a hole which had been filled in with sheets of iron embedded into the ground. He tugged at them and bent them sufficiently to make a gap he was able to slide through.

For almost a year, 'Sandy' Thomas lived in the safety of a Greek monastery in the self-contained and resolutely male community of 8,000 monks. The Germans could not tell him apart.

From Salonika Thomas walked to Athos where he spent a year dodging the Germans before managing to cross the Aegean Sea to safety.

He walked on, trailing the group for a hundred yards or so, then came to a crossroads and struck out on his own. Well before dawn he reached the last outlying suburb and passed a few straggling buildings on the outskirts of the city. He drew his overcoat close around him and walked briskly now in the cold morning air—air that was pure and free.

From here on, Thomas's adventures read like a romance of Walter Scott. For a few days and nights he was sheltered by a family of friendly Greeks, who offered to hide him until the war was over. But the New Zealander reluctantly refused, preferring to attempt the painful walk south to the easternmost of the three fingers of Thrace—Agion Oros—in the hope of jumping a ship to Turkey. On his journey, he encountered other helpful Greeks, and two New Zealanders—Private John Mann, of the 18th NZ Battalion, and Sergeant-Major R H Thompson, DCM, a veteran of Wavell's first Libyan campaign—with whom he stayed for 19 days before continuing his journey to the Holy Mountain of Athos.

Here, for almost a year, he lived among the rocky eyries of the monasteries where no female, human or animal, is allowed. In a strange self-contained community of 8,000 monks, he was shuffled from one monastery to another, dodging the Germans. Finally, after three attempts to cross the stormy Aegean Sea, he reached Turkey in a stolen boat with two Englishmen whom the monks had also sheltered. On reaching Turkish soil, the three men were arrested and thrown into a filthy prison cell, but on the following morning 'two splendid Rolls-Royces' arrived at Police Headquarters and rescued them, bearing them to His Majesty's Consul at Izmir.

Thomas rejoined his division and later became a Regular Officer in the British Army, winning the DSO and MC and Bar.

Now he was in a wide dark grass-covered field, bounded by a high stone wall which was strung copiously with barbed wire, in fact with so many strands that he was able to use them as a ladder. He reached the top without much difficulty, then lowered himself into the shadows.

Within half an hour, he was down in the city, where suddenly he was surrounded by gaiety, with restaurants and bars echoing with the sound of laughter and music. He passed loving couples and inebriated groups of men and street musicians as he wended his way south to reach the foot of the great Salonika Hill.

All the exits to the ancient city were under guard. The southern one divided the city from one of the more modern suburbs. Thomas approached it, keeping to the shadows, then paused. After a time a sentry moved out of the dark archway and shifted his rifle from one shoulder to the other. Presently a group of civilians came straggling down the road toward the gate, happy with drink. He waited until they were converging on the exit and slouched through with them, almost colliding with the sentry.

ESCAPE KITS

Ingenious minds and skilled fingers combined to give potential escapers every chance. Map and compass to plot a route? Break-out tools? Disguises? Forged passes and bribes? The back-room boffins could supply them.

Escaping had a serious aim—to draw German soldiers away from the front—and Allied Forces made great efforts to supply escape materials and give instruction on techniques. But to high-spirited men, escaping could seem like an exciting game and humour was an effective way of informing.

ROYAUME DE BELGIQUE
KONINKRIJK BELGIE

CARTE D'IDENTITE
KAART VAN EENZELVIGHEID

3133

Nom Naam	Van Der Meulen
Prénoms Voornamen	Albert
Etat-civil Burgerstand	célibataire
Nationalité Nationaliteit	Belge
Né à Geboren te	Bruxelles
le den	6 Décembre 1910
Profession Beroep	Ouvrier agricole
Residence Verblijf rue straat	14 Ch.ée de Liége Bruxelles

N° N° **3133**

Inscrit: Vol.
Ingeschreven: Boek **IV**
Fol.
Blad. **346**

Signature du Porteur: *A. Van der Meulen*
Handteeken des Dragers

den **3 Mars 1939**

L'Officier de l'Etat Civil (ou son délégué)
De Ambtenaar van den Burgerlijken (of zijn afgevaardigde)

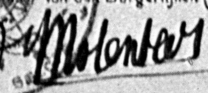

Left False documents were the stock-in-trade of the escaper. Under the Nazi yoke identity cards, travel warrants, work permits, authority to move around—or just to be in a village near a neutral frontier—proliferated. Prisoners bribed or blackmailed guards for examples, information about changes, official marks and so on—then forged their own. They hand copied the typewritten letters—until some one made a wooden typewriter—and cut stamps from potatoes or soft wood.

Right and below Insignia, too, for false uniforms, rolled off the camp production lines. The first stage was to make a mould which could then be used to cast badges and medals. Black and white ribbons that would add the final authentic touch to the imitations of the Iron Cross were sent from Britain—decoratively tied around packets of handkerchiefs.

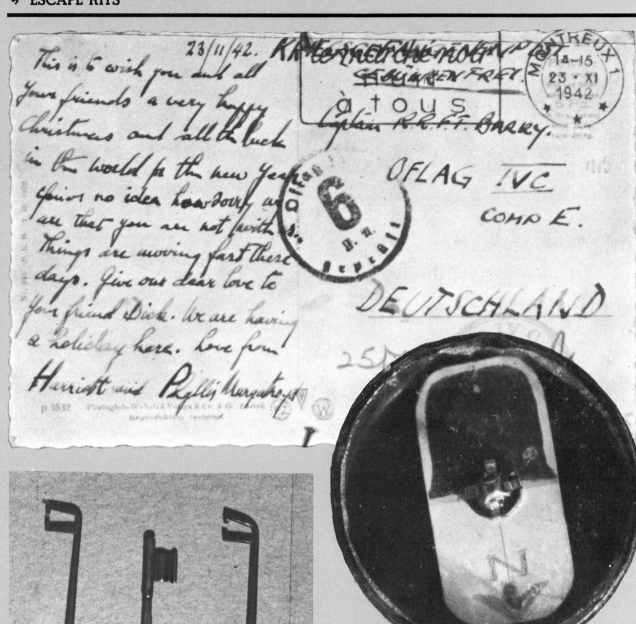

Above Compass construction was a major activity—manufacturers sent out razor blades ready-magnetized, gramophone needles provided the mounts—and virtually anything magnetic that could be persuaded to swing was pressed into service.

Top When the effort paid off with a home-run a coded postcard would revitalize those left behind.

Left Pick locks gave the prisoners in Colditz the run of the castle—particularly after a Gestapo search team had had their master keys stolen.

Right Sets of games sent out from home were stuffed with concealed escape materials—the reply confirmed that they had passed German scrutiny. *Below* Disguise played a great part in would-be escapers' plans. With dies made from ink and some deft re-tailoring an Army uniform would turn into natty city suiting or a dormitory blanket become a Luftwaffe jacket. The trick was to make them look shabby to merge with the worn-out clothing of the Germans. When Captain 'Lulu' Lawton and the other five members of his team walked out of Colditz they were dressed as a German NCO, a German private and four Polish orderlies—in uniforms they had made themselves. This German officer's cap, prepared for another escape attempt, was made by a British prisoner in Colditz.

LICENSED VICTUALLERS SPORTS ASSOCIATION
(WHOLESALE ONLY)

Telephone Central 6952	10, St. Bride Street, London E.C.4.	Secretary J. H. Sherwell

SUPPLIERS OF GAMES AND BAR REQUISITES TO HOTELS, RESTAURANTS, SPORTS CLUBS AND OTHER LICENSED PREMISES

12th May, 1941.

Dear Sir,

Owing to the difficulties in the present situation of obtaining new supplies of sporting goods used in our various Public Houses, Inns, etc., it has been decided by the Association to suspend for the duration of the war our activities in this direction.

Your name has been published as a prisoner of war, and our committee feel that no better purpose can be found for the use of our present stock of goods, than to distribute them to those unfortunate members of the services who are at present in prisoner of war camps.

Accordingly we are despatching to you a parcel of these goods which we hope will reach you in due course in good condition and that you and your colleagues will find them of use.

Should this parcel reach you, your acknowledgement to us would be welcome.

Yours faithfully,

J. H. Sherwell

Secretary.

ACKNOWLEDGEMENT

KRIEGSGEFANGENENPOST

The Secretary
LICENSED VICTUALLERS
SPORTS ASSOCIATION
10 St. Bride Street,
London, E.C.4.

Date. 20th August, '41

Parcel No. 14361 Containing

5 Records.
1 Dart Board.
1 Chess Set.
1 Shovehalfpenny Board.

has been received by me.

(sgd) J. Short, Major.

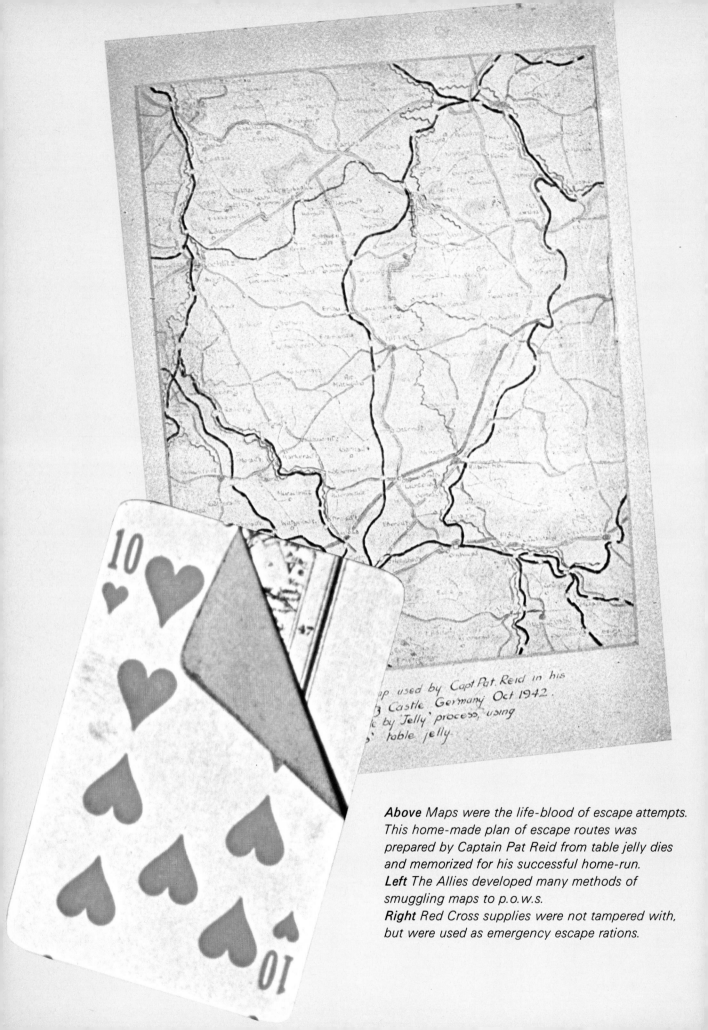

...p used by Capt. Pat. Reid in his
...3 Castle Germany Oct 1942.
...e by 'Jelly' process, using
...' table jelly.

Above Maps were the life-blood of escape attempts. This home-made plan of escape routes was prepared by Captain Pat Reid from table jelly dies and memorized for his successful home-run.
Left The Allies developed many methods of smuggling maps to p.o.w.s.
Right Red Cross supplies were not tampered with, but were used as emergency escape rations.

THE TUNNELLERS

Two hundred escaped prisoners of war loose in the heartland of Germany, drawing divisions of the Wehrmacht from the combat zone where Hitler so desperately needed them—that was the vision of Big X, chief of the escape organization in Stalag Luft III. But the Gestapo took a terrible revenge.

North Compound, Stalag Luft III, had a population of over a thousand, half of whom were RAF and Dominion Air Force officers. And there were about 300 Americans and almost a hundred Poles.

The camp was at Sagan, Germany, a small historic junction town with a chateau, around which the countryside was flat and featureless. South of the town was a forest of fir which ran un-broken towards the Czech frontier. It was on the northern edge of this forest that Stalag Luft III was situated. To build the North Compound a great clearing had been made and the wood-en huts had been built over the tree stumps.

The compound was in the form of a square, nearly a mile in circumference, around which ran two barbed-wire fences seven feet high and seven feet apart. Beyond the outer fence, between 20 and 30 yards away, stood the thick pine forest.

Guarding the perimeter were eight sentry towers, each built 15 feet above the ground and mounted with search-lights and submachine guns. They were spaced around the fences and manned continuously by shifts of sentries.

There were 15 barracks blocks— wooden structures built on blocks one foot above the ground. Each barracks had its own kitchen, washroom and water closets, built on concrete slabs, and at one corner of each room was a heating-stove, also built on a con-

Left 76 prisoners broke out through Harry, the main tunnel dug at Stalag Luft III. Artist and 'forger' Ley Kenyon was sent down the tunnel to record its construction. His original drawings—this one is of the sand trolley on its way from the face—were stored in a sealed canister in Dick, another tunnel, and recovered later.
Top The German camp officers—here taking roll-call—hoped none of the prisoners would want to leave the 'luxurious' North Compound.

crete base. The Commandant, Baron von Lindeiner, considered North Com-pound a luxury camp and had expressed the hopeful view that his prisoners would be so pleased with their new home that they would give up all thought of escaping.

But the Allied prisoners of the North Compound held no such view, being firmly of the belief that it was the duty of every prisoner to try to escape. And to aid them the Compound had set up an escape committee known as Organi-zation X. Its Chief—referred to as 'Big X'—was Squadron Leader Roger Bushell, RAF.

Night came down on Stalag Luft III.

To the German guards on picket duty and guarding the towers, all looked peaceful and normal. The large flat compound, set in a clearing among the fir trees on the northern

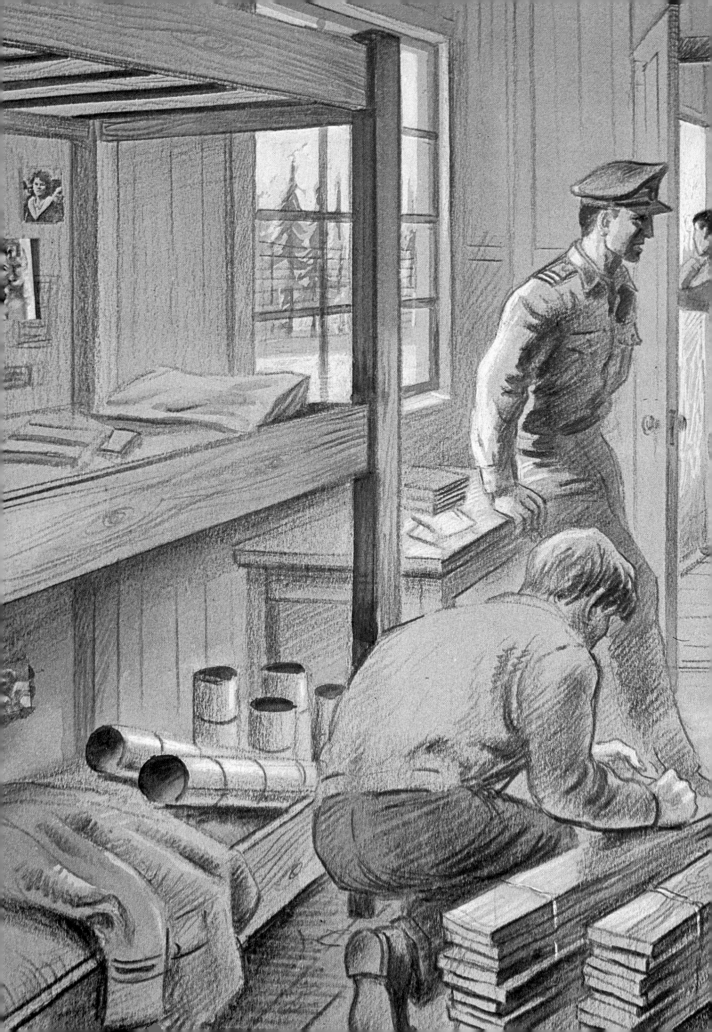

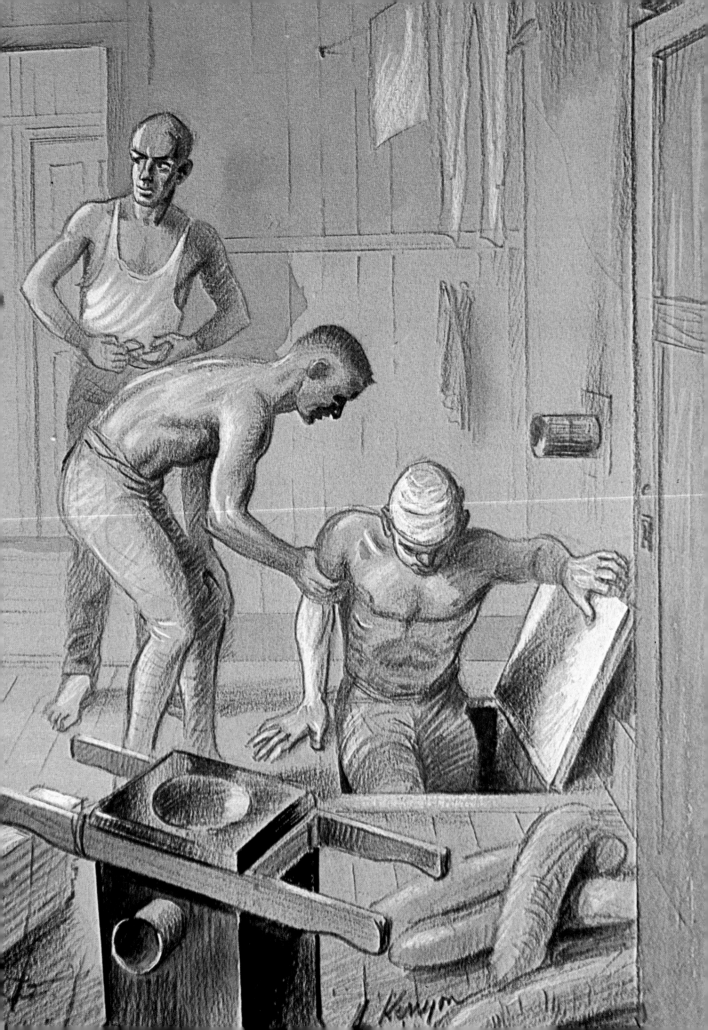

Previous page Ley Kenyon's picture of the small room in Hut 104 from which Harry started is a composite of all that went on—usually there would be as few people as possible in the room. The three diggers moving into the trapdoor entrance are wearing combinations, once in the tunnel they would probably remove even these and work naked. In front of them are trouser-leg bags stuffed with earth from the tunnel that the 'penguins' would scatter about the compound. Ultimately they shifted 500 cubic yards of earth. The trap was normally hidden under the stove here shown shifted away. The boards being tied in bundles came from bunks—Big X, the head of the Escape Organization, made a levy of two slats from every bunk—and were used to shore up the tunnel roof. Before this was done there was always the danger of a fall trapping one of the tunnellers. The tubes are KLIM tins—the dried milk that came in food parcels—ready to extend the air supply system that had its intake behind the wall on the right. In the background a stooge patiently watches for a sign that a German 'ferret' is on the prowl. The system prevented accidental discovery.

fringe of the straggling township, was covered by a thin layer of snow, and the yellow lights that filtered from the rows of windows gave the camp the appearance of a warm and friendly oasis in the stark bleakness of the countryside.

But inside the huts 220 prisoners were making their final acts of commitment. Each, adhering to a carefully worked out schedule, was dressing slowly and pensively, putting on civilian clothes that would make him look like a peasant, a labourer, or a businessman, according to the new identity which had been chosen for him by Organization X. Each man pinned a blanket around him and finally struggled into his greatcoat, then picked up his small piece of hand-luggage, waved farewell to his mates and departed.

One by one, at pre-arranged intervals, they stepped out into the dark bleak compound and moved stealthily through the darkness towards Hut 104 and the entrance to a tunnel called 'Harry'.

By 2100 hours all those who were supposed to be making the break had assembled in the barracks. They stood around in groups, mostly silent, and waited.

The break was supposed to begin at 2130, but it passed, and 2200 came. Nothing seemed to be happening, and nobody knew what was going on. The control officer at the head of the shaft couldn't give out any information because the nearest man was a hundred feet along the tunnel.

But presently he turned and raised a hand,

Left Goon boxes and barbed wire, sentries and machine guns at Stalag Luft III made tunnelling out the sensible way to go.
Below The air pump, installed in a chamber at the base of the shaft, made work below ground much more supportable. As the pumper, sitting on a sliding oarsman's seat, pushed the wooden and wire-framed kit-bag bellows backwards and forwards fresh air flowed along the pipeline.
Right With the air pump working, the trap door could be closed and the stove replaced in position making concealment from a wandering German 'ferret' much easier.

indicating that he had just felt cold air coming up the shaft. He stepped aside for the next man to go down.

The great escape had begun.

Big X and the Big Four

It was an 'X' decision which, in March, 1943, soon after the North Compound was occupied, had set in motion as an official project the simultaneous construction of three escape tunnels.

For security reasons the word 'tunnel' was prohibited from all conversation, and the tunnels were given names—'Tom' was to have its entrance in Hut 123; 'Dick' in 122; and 'Harry' in 104.

Squadron Leader Bushell and his Big Four—Johnny Bull, Johnny Marshall, Wally Floody and 'Crump' Kerr-Ramsay—first made an inspection of Hunt 123, which stood 150 yards from the western boundary wire. In the centre of the building, standing on a concrete base, was the kitchen, and beside it a stove with a chimney. As the location for the entrance to tunnel 'Tom', they chose a badly lit space in a narrow passage next to the stove.

In Hut 122, in the middle of the concrete floor of the washroom, was a sump. It was about eighteen inches square and three feet deep, covered by an iron grating. Into two sides of this square hole ran drain-pipes from the troughs, and out of the third side ran a waste pipe, below which there was a foot of water. The fourth side of the sump was a blank wall.

The Poles, 70-odd of whom occupied this hut, believed they had the answer. A technical team led by Gucio Gutowaki, removed the blank wall of the well and replaced it with a reinforced concrete slab, which could be removed or slid back into place from the top. When in place, the slab could be made waterproof by covering the joins with blue clay mixed with cement. The Big Four enthusiastically endorsed the idea of placing the entrance to tunnel 'Dick' behind the slab in the sump.

'Harry' was even more ingenious. In Hut 104—in the room nearest to the northern boundary—there was a small iron heating-stove in one corner. It stood on a tiled platform about four feet square.

It was decided to remove the stove. Then the tiles were carefully stripped off one by one, after which the whole platform was removed. It was replaced by a solid wooden frame, the top of which was filled in with floorboards. The tiles were then cemented on to the surface.

But it did not pass Big X's inspection. For in the process of building it, five tiles had suffered cracks. Big X sent a note over to East Compound asking for five unbroken tiles. A few days later they arrived, having been taken from the East Camp cook-house.

When the job was finished, the platform looked perfect. One tiny crack was dusted over with cement. Finally, the trap was hinged along one side for quick and easy access.

Moving a mountain of sand

With the first step accomplished successfully in all three cases, the planners were able to concentrate on Phase Two, which was much more dangerous—the digging of the tunnels.

The Germans had sunk sound-detectors at a depth of six feet round the perimeter. To avoid discovery, the planners decided that the tunnels must run 30 feet below the surface of the compound. And the first step in each case was to build a shaft straight down from the entrance to the required depth before starting on the horizontal tunnel. Each of these shafts was shored up with four uprights filled in by wooden slats.

At the bottom of each shaft it was decided to build a complex of small chambers—one to house an air pump, a larger one for storing sand, and a third for use as a workshop.

These proved difficult and dangerous to build in the damp sandy soil, the ceilings having to be shored up as the holes were being excavated. And in 'Dick' there occurred a nasty accident with nearly fatal results.

It happened when Floody, Kerr-Ramsay and 'Conk' Canton were down in the largest chamber putting finishing touches to the walls. Suddenly, Floody gave a cry of warning as a stream of sand began to pour from a space in the ceiling. Canton grabbed up a plank and tried to stem the flow, but it only increased, rapidly filling the hole. They scrambled to the shaft and hauled themselves up the ladder. Floody was caught waist deep in sand and had to be pulled out by the other two.

It had been a close shave, and the situation was extremely dangerous for a time, for it

Organization X turned tunnel building into a major industry. From this tunnel workshop, 30 feet below the ground, poured-digging tools, shoring slats, rail lines and trolleys for shifting sand from the digging face. One prisoner, John Travis, literally carved the wooden wheels of the trolleys and their smooth running wooden ball-bearings by hand. At its peak, Harry had its own electric light supply tapped off from the camp mains.

The workshops also provided a place for the underground shift to rest—digging could be a completely exhausting task.

Organization X backed up their tunnel digging with a supply system that could produce forged documents, 'civilian' clothes, information about German surveillance techniques, escape supplies and rations.

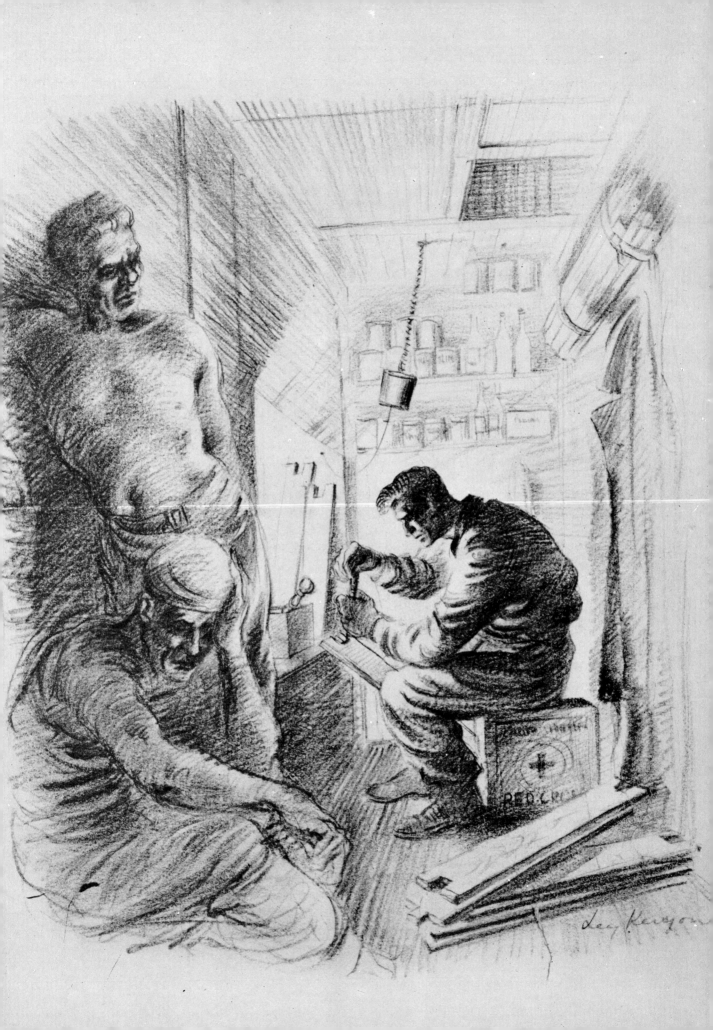

looked as though the whole foundations of the washroom would collapse. But eventually, with extra shoring, the chamber was made ready.

The two main problems were those of shoring and the disposal of excavated sand. Until the entrance shafts had been sunk and enough space was cleared below them, the traps had to be kept open. This meant that excavated sand had to be transported about the camp at times when the German guards were patrolling and the risk of discovery was at its highest. While the shafts were being dug, the sand was hauled up in large metal water jugs, raised and lowered on ropes.

But now the time had come to being work on the horizontal tunnels.

Tunnel 'Tom', from Hut 123, was to be dug due west to reach the fringe of pine trees beyond the fences. 'Dick', from 122, would strike out independently towards the perimeter but might join up with 'Tom' as the project proceeded. 'Harry', from the northern end of Hut 104, would run directly north into the woods, passing directly below the 'cooler' and the roadway.

The sand-dispersers were given the name of 'penguins'. Their job was to collect the soil as it was removed from the shafts and dispose of it secretly within the compound. This called for the utmost caution and considerable ingenuity, for the sandy soil from the tunnels was bright yellow and easily distinguishable from the grey-brown muddy ground of the compound. The three tunnels would ultimately displace some 500 cubic yards of earth, so the penguins had a massive task.

And the shoring. The requirement in wooden slats was in the vicinity of 4,500 square feet!

Heavy engineering

Organization X looked first at the buildings themselves. They found that each of the barracks blocks had a double wooden floor: an upper floor made of planks, and a lower floor of boards about 30 inches long and four to eight inches wide which lay across beams lined with tarred insulation paper to keep out the cold. Another valuable source of shoring timber was

Above and right The four man teams of diggers were backed up by penguins who had to dispose the earth mined. With bags of earth suspended down his trouser legs a penguin could shuffle about the compound dribbling out the bright yellow sand and kicking it into the surface. At one point, 150 penguins were on duty—but when they could hide no more earth the Big Four decided to take the sand from Harry and shovel it into Dick.

the bunks—wooden structures holding two or three tiers, with stout uprights to support the bedframes. Across the frames lay slats from five to eight inches wide.

The bed-slats, being immediately available, went into the construction of the vertical shafts and underground chambers. There were 600 two- or three-tiered bunks in the camp, and Big X made a levy of two slats from each bed. This yielded sufficient timber for the shoring-frames and trap supports. The lower flooring boards were used for lining the tunnels.

Meanwhile, John Travis and Bob Nelson had been working on an air-pump for each shaft. The design had come from a copy of *Popular Mechanics* which someone had found in the prison library. Each pump was made from a bellows attached to a kitbag which was kept distended by four wire hoops sewn inside it, and to which intake and exhaust valves were fitted. The whole unit was mounted on a wooden frame. However, it had to be taken apart and carried underground in sections and re-assembled inside the chamber.

When each tunnel had progressed a dozen or so feet, railways were installed. The rails were lengths of beading strip taken from the barracks blocks and nailed to the tunnel floors, one foot apart. The trucks were wooden boxes with wheels carved from wood and fitted with metal strips cut from old food tins. John Travis, who made them, even fitted the wheel hubs with ball-bearings carved from wood, while to make the axles he removed the iron rods from the cooking stoves. These railways, used for hauling sand along the tunnel floors, pulled along by ropes, saved hundreds of hours of back-breaking work.

Penguins and ferrets

Sand and its disposal continued to be the camp's most pressing problem. The tunnellers in 'Tom' had introduced an evening shift, and to keep up, the penguins had to resort to all kinds of dispersal methods, even to burying some of the sand in garden beds under overturned top soil.

As summer approached, Oberfeldwebel Glemnitz, who was in charge of the 'ferrets', warned his men to maintain even greater vigilance. One of them found some freshly dispersed sand in one of the garden patches. Another, kicking a small pile of earth near the camp theatre, found a patch of the tell-tale yellow sand.

Immediately, Glemnitz put his men on the alert. Barracks were searched daily. The prisoners would come in from *appell* to find their bunks stripped and the whole place turned upside-down. The ferrets crawled under the barracks blocks looking for tunnel entrances. Others chopped down the pine trees that grew inside the compound on the northern side. Others hid

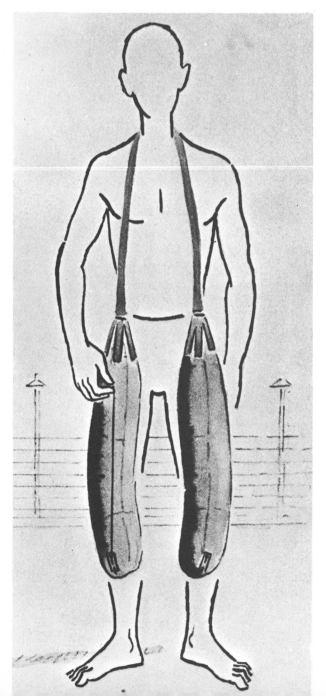

themselves in trees outside the camp and watched the prisoners' movements through field glasses.

They found nothing. And as the days passed, the work below ground went on, and the tunnels grew.

Glemnitz resorted to night raids, reasoning that if nothing could be discovered during the day the prisoners must be working at night. At midnight, at two in the morning, or just before dawn, the prisoners would be awakened by the thud of German jackboots and the sharp order:

'Aus! Aus!'

Cursing under their breaths, the prisoners would drag themselves out of bed, pull a blanket around them and wait while their room was torn apart yet again.

The end of June. July. August. All went well with the three tunnels. 'Tom' had passed beneath the two fences and was reaching out toward the edge of the pine forest.

Then a rumour swept the camp; another new compound was about to be built—to the west,

just where 'Tom' and 'Dick' would come out.

As if to confirm this, some Germans arrived one morning outside the western perimeter with saws and axes and commenced to cut down the pine trees. With the prisoners watching glumly, they felled tree after tree, to make a clearing fifty yards wide and three hundred feet long. 'Tom's' escape hatch would emerge right in the middle of it.

Push on with 'Tom'

Big X decided to push on regardless, and to try to complete 'Tom' as soon as possible. He even sealed up 'Dick' and 'Harry' and pressed on with three shifts to finish the western tunnel before the fences were removed.

But the penguins were in trouble. They had used up every nook and cranny in the camp in dispersing the tons and tons of sand that had been brought to the surface. With long faces they brought their problem to Big X. Roger Bushell called in his Big Four and together they discussed the crisis.

It was Floody who said:

'I've got it. Why not use 'Dick'?'

And that's what they did. 'Dick' was opened up and the penguins carried the excavated sand from the shaft in Hut 123 to the shaft in Hut 122, where workers were waiting to feed it back into the ground.

'Tom' went ahead like wildfire, and to make things easier, a 'halfway house' was built—at a distance of a hundred feet from the entrance shaft. It was a chamber ten feet long, six inches wider than the tunnel and a foot higher, a place where tunnel workers could pass each other. The railway line fed trucks of sand into it from the face, and workers passed them through to the line that would take them to the entrance shaft.

It had become a race now—the diggers trying to complete the tunnel before the Germans could find it. It was now 285 feet long, and the tunnellers estimated that they were beyond the original fringe of trees and needed to go only another few feet before being ready to make the vertical shaft to the surface.

'Tom' is blown

This was the moment when, for some reason, Glemnitz decided that a tunnel was being dug definitely from Hut 123.

His men burst in one day and pulled the place

After the break-out the Germans took photographs of reconstructions of the escape.
Left A German guard climbs out of Harry's exit.
Below To accumulate this tunnelling equipment Organization X stole what it could and bribed and blackmailed the guards for the rest.

apart. But they found nothing. On the following day they came in again and stayed for over three hours, examining every square foot of the barracks. Nothing. They swooped again the following day, and again, and again. Still they found nothing.

Then, by pure chance, some German workmen who were laying a drainpipe outside the entrance to Hut 123 happend to leave a pick-axe lying about. One of Glemnitz's ferrets picked it up as he entered the barracks and began to idly pick away at the concrete floor. While the men in the hut watched, he hit the floor a few more times, and suddenly the point of the pick struck the edge of the trap, where the join had been cemented over. A piece flew off. And the game was up. 'Tom' was discovered.

The Germans were flabbergasted when they went into the tunnel and found out how near it was to completion. They put charges along the length of the tunnel and blew it up.

During the next four months, Organization X sponsored a number of escapes by individuals and small groups. Several prisoners managed to get clear of the Stalag, but all were caught and put back in the camp after a period in the cooler.

'Harry' starts up

Christmas came, and with it the 'off' season for serious escape attempts. Just the time, reasoned Big X, for work to restart on 'Harry', the last remaining tunnel.

On January 10, 1944, the entrance shaft was reopened—it had been so securely sealed that it took the workmen two hours to break it open—and the Big Four took their torches and went down. They found the tunnel intact. The shoring had withstood the weight of the wet earth and had not rotted. Only four frames had to be replaced. But mildew had rotted the canvas of the kitbag used in the airpump, and its pipe was choked with sand. The whole system had to be replaced.

But the overall picture was encouraging. One hundred and twenty feet of the tunnel had been completed, including one halfway house; and

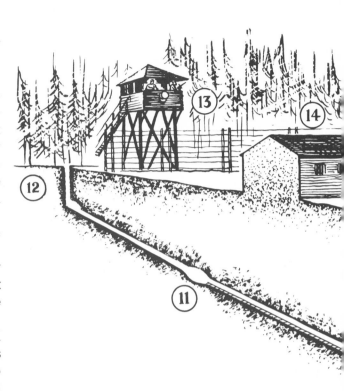

the estimated distance remaining to be dug to bring the tunnel to the trees beyond the fences was a further 220 feet. Two more halfway houses would have to be built.

It took five days to make the tunnel safe for the diggers, and work was resumed on January 15.

Once again, the disposal of excavated sand became a major problem. Snow now covered the compound, and the sand could no longer be dispersed over the surface.

The theatre provided the answer. It had been built by the prisoners, and they remembered the spaces beneath the tiered seating in the auditorium. It would be ideal.

But the theatre was at the end of the compound, and a stream of prisoners to and from it in the daytime would have been noticed. Consequently, the work was done by relays of men each night before 2200 hours.

The work went on, and January passed. A full moon caused a break in the dispersal activities for a few nights, after which the work continued.

An acute shortage of electric cable had thus far limited the lighting in the tunnel to a single bulb at the base of the entrance shaft. But one

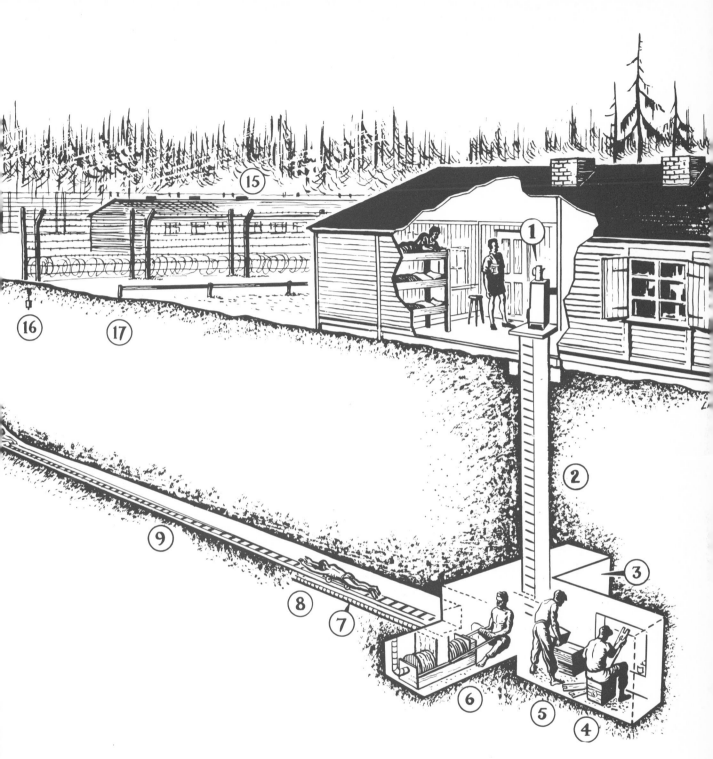

When finished Harry was an impressive piece of work. **1** Stove over trap door **2** Shaft **3** Workshop and storage space **4** Making the shoring frames **5** Wooden sand boxes **6** Air pump **7** KLIM tin air line **8** Tunneller on trolley **9** Rail lines **10** and **11** Halfway houses **12** Exit shaft **13** Goon box **14** Cooler or prison block **15** Outside barbed wire **16** Sound detector **17** Inner warning wire morning a Canadian officer returning from a brief spell in the camp cooler noticed a German up a pole laying an overhead power line. On the ground lay a large coil of red insulated cable. The Canadian scooped it up and delivered it into Hut 104. The German electrician, afraid at having lost the cable, refrained from reporting the loss. The coil contained over 800 feet of cable, and it was put to good use. From this time onwards, the tunnellers had the benefit of a light in each of the halfway houses and at the working face, all powered from the mains supply.

The tunnel passed the 200 foot mark by mid-February, and the second halfway house was installed. Another new moon came and went.

And then it was learned that Glemnitz was to go on two weeks leave on March 1. Big X decided that the tunnel should be completed before he returned.

But the chief ferret must have had his ear to the ground. For on March 1, at morning *appell*, twenty prisoners, including several key tunnellers and security men associated with 'Harry', were called out of the ranks and informed that they were being transferred to Belaria Camp, three miles away. They were summarily sent off without even being able to return to their barracks to pick up their belongings.

But the remaining diggers pressed on with greater energy than ever, and during the next nine days dug and shored up 112 feet of tunnel, including the third and last halfway house.

The exit shaft

There now remained only the exit shaft.

This proved extremely difficult and quite dangerous. The digger had to work upwards, above his head, with the loose sand falling down on him. And there was always the danger of a big fall of earth.

The carpenters put in special shoring, and provided a shield consisting of a frame of three boards, one of which could be removed at a time. As the exit shaft grew in height, a ladder was fitted in sections.

When the shaft was 20 feet high, Kerr-Ramsey went up the ladder armed with an old fencing foil, which he used as a probe. It was night, and he knew that if the point of the foil broke the surface it would not be noticed in the dark. He gently pushed the foil upwards into the soil until it ceased to meet with any resistance. He found to his amazement that the surface above the shaft was only nine inches away!

He came down and reported the exciting news to the carpenters who were standing by, and they built a platform at the top of the shaft to support the soil in case a roving picket should accidentally tread on the spot and fall through. It was 2145 hours on March 14. The last shift climbed out of the entrance shaft. Then the carpenters sealed down the trapdoor. Tunnel 'Harry' was ready.

On March 15, the action committee of Organization X met to discuss the possible date for the escape. Weather was the all-important factor, and a moonless night was the first requirement. Also, a strong wind, to cover odd noises like the snap of twigs or the scrape of feet.

The nearest moonless nights, the Met. Officer told them, would be Thursday, Friday and Saturday—March 22, 23 and 24.

There were other considerations. Fewer trains would run through Sagan on Sunday, March 25. Therefore, Saturday was out. The ideal night for the escape was Friday, March 23. And this was the date tentatively set, although the Escape Committee, when putting it forward, reserved the right to postpone the break for a further month should conditions turn out to be not completely favourable.

Ready to go

During the week leading to X-Day, preparations went ahead smoothly. Tailors, forgers, cooks and instrument-makers were at work manufacturing and perfecting the hundreds of items which would be needed in a mass escape.

In all the cook-houses in the camp, iron rations were being prepared. Grated chocolate, oatmeal, crushed biscuits, vitamin pills, sugar, milk powder and other concentrated foods were

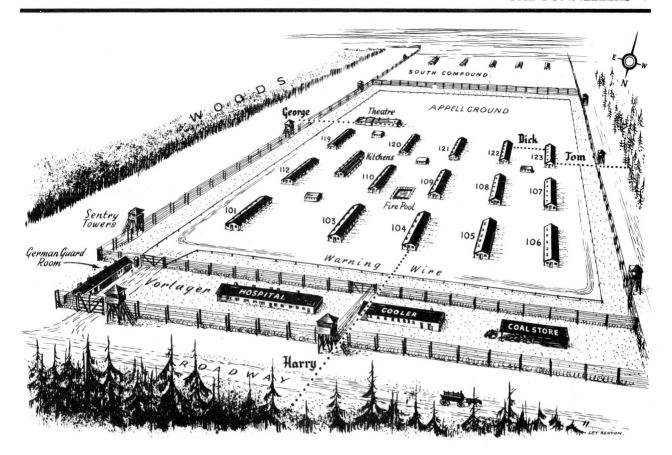

boiled and baked into a heavy nourishing fudge, which was packed into four ounce cocoa tins.

Suitcases were collected or manufactured. Compasses were made by the instrument makers.

Electricians installed extra lighting throughout the length of the tunnel—eight bulbs every 25 feet—and came out announcing that 'Harry' was now lit up like Broadway.

Blankets were spread over the floor of the tunnel near each end to deaden the sound of movement, and more blankets were laid beneath the halfway houses so that trolley haulers working in them wouldn't get their clothes soiled. Planks about five feet long were nailed to the trolley frames so that escapers would be able to lie on them as they were being hauled through with their luggage. Below the sound detectors the railway lines were covered with strips of blanket to muffle the sound of the wheels. And blankets were hung across the end of the last halfway house to prevent light from the tunnel from being reflected up the shaft.

At last the day dawned—Friday, March 23— X-Day.

There had been some snow during the night

Tom was blown by the Germans, Dick was closed down, Harry going straight out under the cooler and the main roadway was the one that got away. The Gestapo thought retribution would prevent further escape attempts: the prisoners retaliated by starting George from the theatre.

and the weather was still unsettled, with a chilly wind from the east. A conference was called at 1130 hours, when the decision to proceed was taken. Within a few minutes every man in the North Compound knew that the escape was on.

Shortly after lunch, the leader of every block called his escapers together and briefed them. Then they were issued with rations, water-bottles, compasses and maps, clothing and other items.

During the afternoon, a team worked in the tunnel to give it the finishing touches. And members of the Forgery Section worked against the clock filling in dates on nearly 500 forged papers. And every escaper made a final check of his equipment.

Evening roll-call—and the atmosphere so

electric that it seemed certain something must happen to alert the Germans. But it passed without incident, and the men broke up into groups and filed back into their barracks.

Last-minute hitch

The hold-up had been at the escape hatch. Johnny Bull had climbed up the ladder to remove the boards holding the layer of earth, to find them so tightly wedged in it was impossible to move them. After 20 minutes of sweating and cursing, he came down the ladder and admitted defeat. Johnny Marshall stripped off and went up to have a try. Eventually, after several more minutes, he prised the first board loose and tugged it away. The others came out easily. Then Bull went up and scraped away the last few inches of soil. His handspade broke through and ice-cold air hit his perspiring face. As he scooped away the rest of the earth he saw the dark sky dotted with faint stars. He slowly eased himself up the ladder and put his head out.

To his horror he found himself out in the open. Instead of being just inside the edge of the forest, the hole was sitting in clear flat ground— with the sentry-box only 15 feet away! And it was only a few steps from the path taken by the roving pickets. He went down the ladder to the end halfway house and broke the news in a hoarse whisper.

Nothing daunted, they decided that the escape must go on. There was no choice. The snow had stopped, and the escape hole would be discovered in the morning for certain.

Bull went up the ladder. He climbed out, spread a folded blanket on the snow and lay on it, facing the camp. From here he watched the tower and the perimeter. There were no guards in sight.

The next man, Marshall, was already standing on the ladder, just out of sight. Bull tapped him on the shoulder and he climbed out. It was his job to take a rope, one end of which was tied to the top rung of the ladder, and to tie the other end to a tree about 70 yards inside the wood. This was to guide the succeeding escapers to

Above This German photograph looking up Harry from the base of the shaft shows the blankets nailed over the rails to ensure that the trolleys would run silently.
Right A German soldier squeezes from Harry's exit: it was so inconspicuous that a guard who stood close by to urinate while the escape was in progress noticed nothing.

the assembly point, from where, in small parties, they would move away from the camp.

Having fixed the rope in place, Marshall gave it a tug. This was to tell Bull that it had been done. The next man, Valenta, was waiting on the ladder, but Bull held him back.

A German soldier was approaching from the west along the boundary wire. He came silently along, reached the sentry tower, and turned back. Another guard reached the tower from the east, turned and walked back. The man in the tower played his searchlight along the barbed wire of the boundary fences and criss-crossed it over the compound.

Valenta came out, pushing his case ahead of him. He crawled across the snow, keeping contact with the rope, and disappeared in the darkness of the woods. Big X, himself, was next—Bushell, who spoke French and German fluently, was travelling as a French worker. His running mate was Scheidhower, a Dutchman.

Then came Flight-Lieutenant Walenn, the man who ran the forgery section, followed by Marcinkus, a Lithuanian RAF officer. Together they made for the Czech border.

Taking off

Back in Hut 104, the tension was mounting. There were twice the usual number of men standing around and lolling on the bunks, and stooges had stationed themselves around the block to give warning of approaching Germans.

They made a queer looking lot—well-dressed businessmen, labourers, artisans—even two in German uniforms.

The endless delays had frayed their nerves, and someone had put on some gramophone records to pass the time and keep a normal atmosphere. Some of them surreptitiously stole a look at the railway timetables which had been smuggled into the compound. Each man knew what train he was to catch, and what alternative trains there were if he were running late. But gradually hopes began to fade as they realized that if the present rate continued the number of escapers would be cut by half!

Then—just before midnight the lights went out.

The distant drone of planes told the prisoners why: there was an RAF raid on Berlin, and the camp had been plunged into darkness.

Organization X had foreseen such an emergency. A number of margarine lamps had been prepared. They were brought out of their

hiding place, lit, and passed along the tunnel to the half-way houses. But another half-hour had been lost.

In one way the blackness into which the Stalag had been plunged was a blessing in

Ley Kenyon's drawing shows the scene as the escapers set off into the blackness. Each one followed the rope stretching from Harry's exit to a marshalling point in the wood then kept watch and tugged on the rope when all was clear for the next man. Only then would he move off into the wood.

disguise. The officer controlling the mouth of the tunnel was able to allow the men to leave without any hold-ups. The men came through one by one, felt their way along the rope to the point of departure, and went on their way.

The lights came on again. The bombers had gone and the countryside was silent again.

A few more men came through. A large case caused a further hold-up—and knocked some shoring frames out of place, causing a fall of earth inside the tunnel. Operations were halted while two tunnellers went down and put them back into place and brought out the sand.

It had wasted 50 minutes of precious time.

But the escape went on—at the rate of one man every ten minutes.

By now it had become evident that less than half the estimated number of escapers would have the chance of making the break, and a hundred of them were ordered to take their gear back to their huts and go to bed. It was a depressing anti-climax for them.

At 0400 there was another hold-up. There was a change of guard among the sentries patrolling the perimeter. The control officer stopped the prisoners from coming through until the new shift had come on and been marched off.

All clear. The controller tapped the next man on the shoulder. He climbed out, crawled into the forest and was gone.

Discovered?

At 0430 a voice cut through the stillness and alarmed the escapers at the north of the shaft. A German guard called from the tower overlooking the road. A sentry who was passing the entrance climbed up into the tower. After a brief whispered conversation, the man who had called out came down the ladder and strolled across the road on to the clearing and made directly for the mouth of the tunnel. He stopped within four feet of the shaft, beside which the controller was lying, holding his breath and clutching the shoulder of the man waiting at the head of the ladder. While the controller died a thousand deaths, the German guard unhurriedly relieved himself on to the snow-covered ground, steam from the stream of urine rising with an acrid smell. He rebuttoned his flies and strolled back to the tower and climbed the ladder. Then the sentry climbed down and strolled off.

Just before 0450 the sky in the east had begun lighten and the last ten men to be allowed through had begun their escape. Lang was controlling; an air-gunner named Carter climbed out and crawled along beneath the rope to the departure tree. He paused there, as leader of the last ten-man party.

Next came a Canadian named Ogilvie. Then Shand, a New Zealander. Following him came Squadron Leader Len Trent, VC, DFC.

At this moment Lang gave the rope two sharp tugs and punched the shoulder of McBride, who was waiting on the ladder below him.

A German sentry was strolling towards them. He was coming along the perimeter, well out from the second fence, a silent shadow moving through the gloom, and apparently deep in thought or half asleep.

They waited, frozen to the snow-covered ground. The sentry came on. He was ten yards away. Six. Five. His foot missed the hole by an

1. Birkland, H.
2. Brettell, E.G.
3. Bull, L.
4. Bushell, R.J.
5. Casey, M.J.
6. Catanach, J.
7. Christensen, A.G.
8. Cochran, D.H.
9. Cross, I.J.
10. Espelid, H.
11. Evans, B.H.
12. Fuglesang, N.
13. Gouws, J.S.
14. Grisman, W.J.
15. Gunn, A.
16. Hake, A.H.
17. Hall, C.P.
18. Hayter, A.R.H.
19. Humphreys, E.
20. Kidder, G.A.
21. Kierath, R.V.
22. Kiewnarski, A.
23. Kirby-Green, T.G.
24. Kolanowski, A.W.
25. Krol, S.

Of the 76 officers who escaped three reached England. Of the recaptured remainder the Gestapo shot 50—one by one with a single bullet in the back 'while attempting to escape'. This picture of half those shot shows Big X himself at no. 4— Squadron-Leader Roger Bushell.

inch. His next step grazed Lang's elbow. He went past, took another step, then stopped. He swung about, his rifle whipped across his waist—

'Nicht schiessen!' Carter shouted, from the tree—German for 'Don't shoot!'

The German, startled out of his wits, jerked his gun around at him and fired.

Shand sprang to his feet and, bending low, ran into the forest. Ogilvie threw away his kit and followed him. Carter, hands above his head, stayed where he was, while Trent and Lang got to their feet.

The sentry had recovered from the first shock. He flashed his torch onto the faces of the prisoners and took out a whistle and blew it shrilly. McBride, hands raised, climbed out of the shaft and stood beside the others. Meanwhile, the guard in the tower was frantically telephoning the guardhouse.

Of the remainder, 13 were captured— five being returned to Stalag Luft III, three to the Air Force camp at Barth, and five to Sachsenhausen concentration camp.

And 50 officers were caught and murdered by the Germans—ostensibly while resisting arrest—on direct orders from Hitler.

But if this terrible retribution had been exacted with the object of frightening the North Compound out of further escape attempts, the Germans had made a psychological blunder. Within a couple of months, a reformed Organization X was working on a tunnel which was directed under the theatre. Its name was 'George'.

Of the 76 prisoners who escaped, three reached England. Two of these were Pilot Officer J. E. Miller and Sergeant P. Bergsland, both Norwegians of the RAF. They travelled by train to Stettin, where they contacted some French workers who smuggled them aboard a ship to Sweden. They reached Stockholm on March 30 and England a week later. The other man, Flight Lieutenant B. van der Stock, travelled by train to Holland, then to Belgium, where he was put into the hands of the Underground Organization. He was sent by train to Toulouse, then through Spain to Gibraltar, and finally was flown back to England.

SURVIVAL
IN YUGOSLAVIA

Bombed, shot up, force marched, somewhere in the middle of a four-sided battle between Germans, Partisans, Chetniks and Americans—the crew of a US Air Force Liberator bailed out over Yugoslavia and survived a year so far behind the lines that they slept in the same rooms as German soldiers!

At 0900 hours on July 28, 1944, more than 200 Liberators of the US Fifteenth Air Force were strung out over the Adriatic, their destination Ploesti, Hitler's greatest European-based oil-source. Because of its distance from the Middle East air-bases and the massive anti-aircraft installations and the numerous fighter squadrons that dotted the route, Ploesti was the roughest target in Europe.

In the second of three flights from the 776th Bombardment Squadron was a B-24 flown by Lieutenant Lewis Perkins. His gunners test-fired their guns into the sea, and his navigator, Lieutenant James Inks, kept busy warning Perkins of the formation's turns and climbs. Presently they were over Yugoslavia at 24,000 feet, and a jigsaw puzzle of tiny towns and villages and green and brown fields inched below.

At 1030 Inks reported:

'Ploesti less than 60 miles.'

As they approached the target he folded the RO table and helped Morley, the bombardier, to set the intervalometer. Now they flew straight and steady. The bomb-bay doors were open. The whole crew sweated out the flak as the bomber made its run.

'Bombs away!'

The Liberator disgorged its load and seemed to float up with buoyancy. Perkins put the nose down and banked at full bore, turning sharply for home. At that instant an enormous blast filled the plane. It seemed to stop, shuddering and quaking, in mid-air. Then it wobbled and began to slide over on one wing as the crew made for the exit.

Previous pages and opposite As Lieutenant Lewis Perkins of the American 776th Bombardment Squadron dropped his 8,000-pound bomb-load on the refineries at Ploesti, Rumania, Hitler's greatest oil source, his aircraft was almost blasted from the sky. For some of the crew—such as Lieutenant James Inks pictured standing third from the left in front of a B-24 on the page before—it was the prelude to an adventure that took them across Yugoslavia.

Morley, the bombardier, baled out. Pizion, the waist-gunner followed him. Number One engine was pouring out oil and gas. Perkins feathered the prop. The Liberator was flying straight and level. There was a chance that they could stagger home on three engines.

The crew tossed out everything they could to lighten the load. Their ammunition went first, then the ten .50 in.-calibre machine-guns. Flak suits, cameras, gun mounts went next. Two hours later, they were still flying, all alone in the bright blue sky.

We're not going to make it

At 1312 Perkins said to Inks:

'We're not going to make it. Plot a course to nearest friendly territory.'

Inks looked at his maps. They were heading back across Yugoslavia. He remembered what the Intelligence Officer had told them at the briefing: no-where east of the Adriatic was safe, but Montenegro was overrun by guerrillas who were friendlier than the Jerries.

At 1342, on a heading toward the northern tip of Albania, the crew began to bale out . . .

As James Inks neared the earth he heard the sound of rifle-shots and the stutter of machine-guns all around him. He hit the ground with a jolt that jarred his back, and both legs crumpled under him. He lay stunned for a time, then roused himself, pulled the chute in, bundled it up and hid it in the scrub.

A bullet zinged past his ear and he threw himself flat. Shooting seemed to come from all around him. He got to his feet and started running, crouched double, stumbling over the rocky ground, weaving between the low scrub-covered hills. Finally, exhausted, he threw himself into a crevice and lay there, gulping in great lungfuls of air.

The shots faded into the distance and his heart-beats and breathing became easier. He began to wonder about the other members of the crew . . .

'Hands oop!'

The voice was deep. It came from close behind him. He turned to see a bearded man,

short and stocky, who was pointing a rifle at his stomach. He obeyed, and marched where he was told. They entered a rocky ravine—where he found five other members of the Liberator crew.

Perkins, Aclan, Schuffert, Griffin and McCormick were standing with their hands up, surrounded by a score or so of short, stocky men wearing what appeared to be home-made attempts at a uniform—tight-fitting trousers, a short jacket, an overseas cap, all cut apparently from grey horse-blankets. There was a small circular silver emblem on their caps.

An NCO gave an order and the Americans were led along a tortuous path which gradually swung northwards into the mountains. They stumbled on, stopping briefly for meals, until five o'clock the following morning when they reached a mountain peak and went a short distance down the other side to find a small timber house. It was surrounded by a hundred or more soldiers.

Friends of America

They were taken into the house and paraded before a tall bearded man with a striking presence. He was the guerrillas' Supreme Commander of All Montenegro.

'You are not prisoners', he assured them. 'We are Chetniks and friends of America. We will get you to Italy in boat.'

Chetniks were royalists, faithful to their king, who was exiled in England. They had fought the Nazis with Allied assistance, which included supplies, men and money. But when Russia came into the war, the Allies shifted their allegiance to another guerrilla group called the Partisans, led by Tito. The Partisans were the enemy of the Chetniks, who were now allied with the Germans as a means of self-protection from the Communists. To complicate matters still further, there was a third group—the Utashi—who were Nazis, and who fought against both the Chetniks and the Partisans.

Arky turned up a day later. The only two missing were Morley and Pizion, who had both jumped over Ploesti. Lieutenant Perkins and his crew were joined by another American flier, the lone survivor of a B-24 that had been shot down three months before. He was Lieutenant Delbert Peterson, and he went wild at meeting them.

The Liberator crew learned that they had parachuted into the middle of a large-scale skirmish between the Chetniks and the Partisans!

They appeared to be safe enough here, although the guerrillas looked at them curiously and with unveiled suspicion. But then they heard that the Nazis, on finding the wrecked Liberator, but no bodies, had posted a reward for the capture of the American crew—a reward of $50,000.

The Americans learned this from a Chetnik captain, who told them, smiling, that the money would be paid whether they were taken dead or alive. Whether or not someone turned them in they never heard, but within a few weeks the Germans came looking for them. In a long game of hide-and-seek, the Chetniks moved them from camp to camp along rugged chasms and precipitous mountains covered with beech, pine and alpine scrub.

Late in September there were rumours that the Allies had taken Paris and were giving the Germans a hard time in Greece and Albania. The Jerries began to pull out of all the surrounding outposts, leaving the Chetniks to hold vast tracts of country against the Partisans.

The American fliers decided that it was time to make a break for the coast, and they split up into three groups—Perkins, Schuffert and Spain; Inks, Arky, Griffin and McCormick; and Peterson and Aclan.

Guerillas all

Inks' group, the largest, decided that their ragged uniforms looked sufficiently like the

Previous B-24 raids had created fearsome damage. When four of the shot-down American fliers found themselves in the shattered Yugoslav town of Podgorica they had to keep quiet the fact that they had bombed the town only three weeks before. Here are typical 776th sorties.

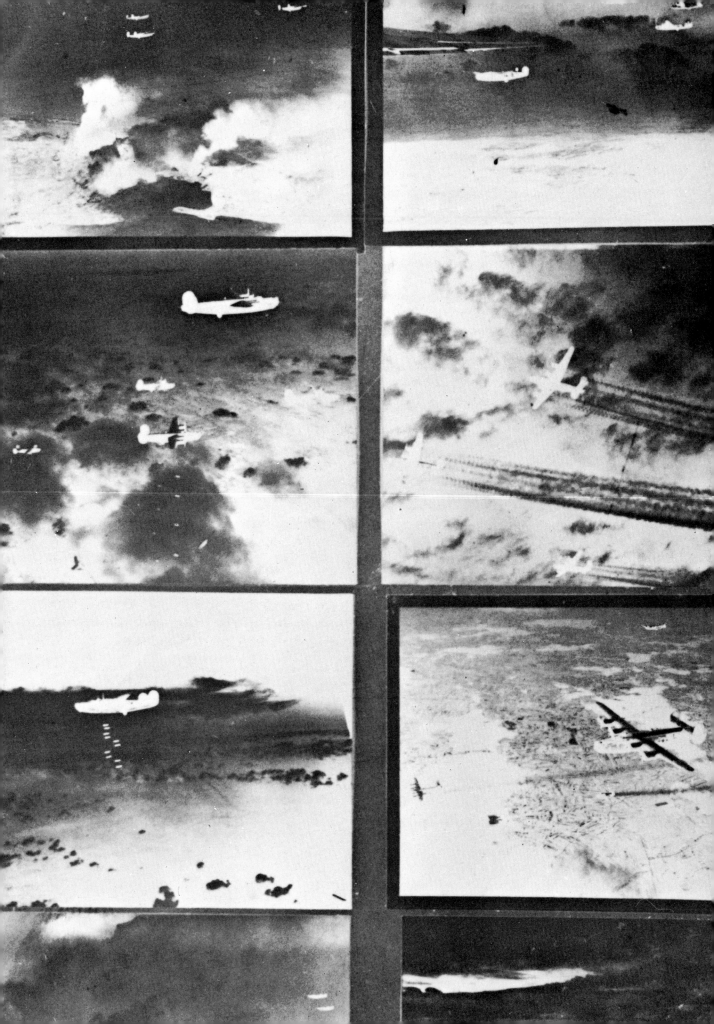

Chetniks' for them to pretend that they were members of the guerrilla group. They scrounged rifles, packs and caps and joined a group of two dozen Chetniks who were heading for Podgorica.

There were hundreds of civilian refugees on the road, and the group mingled with them. German troops were everywhere, and truck convoys roared through at regular intervals.

Late in the afternoon, they came to a roadblock. There were four German soldiers guarding it, checking the papers of each refugee. More Germans stood at the side of the road and behind the barricade. Barbed wire fences stretched across the fields on either side. The Chetnik major in charge of the Americans' party went ahead and spoke to the Germans, then turned and waved them through.

The Americans were walking on the left side of the road between two lines of Chetniks. The four German guards were spaced across the opening so that the guerrillas had to pass between them, single file. The fliers passed between two Germans and marched on down the road, realizing with relief that they must look like part of the scenery. They were safe.

Further on there were Germans all around, mostly small groups of infantry and men from anti-aircraft units, camped in hundreds of puptents in the fields on each side of the road. Rows of them were sitting by the side of the road, and they watched the ragged band of guerrillas pass with a mixture of curiosity and amusement.

Just on sundown they reached another roadblock and passed through it without question. As light was fading, they reached the outskirts of Podgorica. They found a haystack in a field close to the road and fell into it, exhausted.

Next morning they went into the town. It had been heavily damaged by Allied bombing. The Americans kept to themselves the fact that they had taken part in a heavy raid on Podgorica three weeks before they were shot down. They looked at block after block of shattered buildings and wondered which of them had been hit by their own bombs.

The Jerries were everywhere. They milled through the bomb-torn streets, fully in charge, drilling, working, moving vehicles filled with troops and stores, and setting up command posts and communications.

The guerrilla party moved right through the town and out to a village about 15 miles further on. They were given quarters in a school house which had been taken over by the Chetniks. The Americans were given space in a room shared by the camp commandant, Captain Vlado, and his adjutant.

Aclan rejoined them here, and they heard the bad news that Perkins, Schuffert and Spain had been killed. (The news was untrue.) Peterson and Aclan had reached the sea. They had boarded a boat and were sneaking out of the harbour just before dawn, when a German machine-gun opened up on them. Four Chetniks were killed and two wounded. Both Americans dived overboard and escaped. They learned later that Peterson had escaped inland and was hidden by a Montenegro family somewhere along the coast.

By November, the Allies were driving the Germans out of Greece. They were retreating through Albania. The Russians were pushing down from Belgrade, and with the Albanians attacking from the rear, the Germans were fighting to break out of the trap. The Partisans had the Montenegro Chetniks practically surrounded.

Top Sergeant McCormick, here with his parents, threaded his way with four other American fliers through the war-time chaos of Yugoslavia.
Left In Lieutenant Ink's own notation: this is the crew I went down with except the ones standing and kneeling on the right. I replaced their navigator (standing) and Schuffert their radio operator (kneeling). Standing, left to right, Morley, Perkins, Aclan; kneeling, McCormick, Umfleet, Pizion, Griffin and Spain.

Allies of the Germans!

As the days passed, the Germans closed ranks with the Chetniks for last-ditch survival. They even moved into the school house, and the little group of Americans found themselves in an unenviable and unbelievable position. They were being bombed by their own planes, which

were daily and nightly battering the German installations and convoys. And they were living cheek by jowl with the Germans, sleeping in the same room as them, and sharing food with them, and having to keep on guard from being revealed as Americans!

There was nothing else they could do. There was nowhere to run to. The Germans were regrouping, planning to fight their way through the Partisans and the Russians and break out in the north towards Germany. The Americans' only hope was to stay with the Chetniks and let the Partisans capture them.

Each night the sound of the fighting grew closer. And each day the Allied planes bombed and strafed the shrinking perimeter. The Partisans now attacked continuously with mortar, small-arms and grenades. The Germans and Chetniks flung them back time after time—with the Jerries' artillery and the Chetniks' snipers.

Food was extremely scarce now, and it was only a question of how long they could hold out. An American dollar brought hundreds of Reichs-marks, but the Reichsmark bought nothing. With little food, and nights without sleep, the handful of Americans were haggard, red-eyed and desperate.

On November 27, they moved out with a small party of Chetniks on a flat-bed truck. Winding and jolting into the hills, they moved through marching columns of German troops and convoys of vehicles. There were Allied planes in the sky almost continuously now, and time after time the men had to jump from the truck and dive for cover to shelter from flights of strafing US P-38s.

Americans v. Americans

In one attack, Inks found himself sharing a ditch with a bunch of Germans. Three Lightnings came swooping in, their .50-calibres chopping

After every raid intelligence officers 'debriefed' the returning American crews. An Intelligence officer had told Inks: 'No-where east of the Adriatic is safe: but the Yugoslav guerillas might be friendlier than the Jerries.'

up the earth in a straight line towards them. Inks jammed the clip into his rifle and brought it up to fire. But before he could get in a shot, the planes were gone, and he lay trembling among the Germans, some of them dead and wounded, and quaked with tension and relief. He had tried to shoot at an American plane!

On the morning of December 2, the Americans decided to go it alone. Just after daybreak, they stole away from the Chetnik camp and scouted the valley, carrying a pillowcase tied to a stick as a white flag. They took all the food they could buy or beg—rice, beans and potatoes—and headed for the rocks. When they reached there they sat among the boulders to watch the Allied fighters and fighter-bombers tearing the German convoys to pieces.

There was no easy way out, and for weeks they moved from hiding-place to hiding-place. When it snowed heavily in the mountains, they had to come down to the road to try and get food. And here they found themselves trapped in the midst of a full-scale retreat.

There were vehicles of every description, powered by gasoline, oil, paraffin, charcoal;

tanks—8,000 of them, lumbering on until their fuel ran out, or until they were blasted by a strafing fighter; jeeps, command cars, limousines; carts, pulled by old men and women and children. Horses, donkeys, mules, goats, dogs—and human beings.

Incredibly, the Americans survived, but only by rejoining Chetnik units and staying with them. One day in mid-February, they reached Zvornik, to find it swarming with German troops. The Germans had built a pontoon bridge across the river and their troops were crossing it, leaving the Chetniks behind.

In the evening, the little group of ragged, half-starved Chetniks and Americans stopped by the side of the road to rest. The Americans, relieved by finally saying good-bye to the Germans, were talking more freely than they had in months, when a tall, broad-shouldered Chetnik major came over to them.

'Are you Americans?' he asked incredulously, in perfect English. When they replied that they were, he continued:

'Come with me. I will take you to your countrymen.'

The Americans leapt to their feet. The major took them to General Mihailovich's head-quarters, which was a two-storey house nearby.

The guerilla fighters of Yugoslavia were brave men involved in a confusing tug of loyalties. The Chetniks—the group the American fliers first found themselves with—were royalists, faithful to their exiled king and friends of America. But the Allies gave their allegiance to Tito and his Partisans and the Chetniks, to survive, had to fight with the Germans. After the Germans finally abandoned the Chetniks, the American fliers made their way to the Partisans and eventually home.

Left The journey home lasted nearly a year for Aclan, Arky, Griffin and McCormick and took them through some of the most confusing fighting of World War II. Astonishingly the Americans survived battles between Chetniks and Germans, Germans and above Partisans, Chetniks and Partisans—and even strafing by their own American planes.

And here they met five other Americans and an Englishman, all fliers who had been shot down over Yugoslavia.

That evening, the Chetnik chief sent a radio message to the Fifteenth Air Force in Italy to arrange for their evacuation.

The message went late in February 1945. But the American fliers soon discovered that because of the complicated political situation they were by no means safe. There followed a series of signals instructing them to join the Partisans. But the Partisans were harassing the Chetniks every night, and to attempt to approach them wearing Chetnik uniforms would have been suicide. Incredibly, it was not until late in May, after a further series of hardships and escapes, that Inks and the other surviving members of the Liberator's crew were able to put themselves safely into Partisan hands, and then only when the war in Europe finally ended, with the Germans surrendering and the Chetniks dispersing to the mountains.

After escaping by train to Banja Luka during a fierce skirmish between the two guerrilla groups, the Americans hitch-hiked by train and truck to Brod, where Tito's men took them to a hotel. They were then taken by train to Belgrade, where they were handed over to the US Mission to Tito and later flown to Italy.

71

ESCAPE FROM HELL CAMP

The Nazi's top-security prison camp, close to Germany's Polish border, held RAF officers in a fanatically-disciplined prison-within-a-prison. For Warrant Officer Pape the only way out was a complete change of identity—and a transfer to the even harsher conditions of labour in the Polish coalmines.

On September 7, 1941, Warrant Officer Richard Pape, a tough red-headed navigator of an RAF Stirling heavy night bomber, was shot down over Holland while returning from a bombing raid over Berlin. After working with the Dutch underground and evading capture for several months, he was captured and sent to Dulag Luft. *Here, he was labelled a recalcitrant troublemaker and transferred to* Stalag VIIIb, *near Breslau, Germany's largest top-security prison camp.*

The journey from Dulag Luft had taken three nights and four days. The train had halted at numerous sidings for wearisome intervals, and the Allied prisoners, locked in freezing and comfortless cattle trucks, were a sick lot, hungry, dispirited and at the end of their tether.

Rain was falling as the long drab train clanked to a halt at Annaberg, near Breslau. After an interminable wait the prisoners were herded on to the siding under a heavy guard and split up into squads of four, each in the charge of a dour steel-helmeted guard armed with a rifle with fixed bayonet.

They were marched in sullen silence under a grey sky for a distance of five miles. The road passed through a vast gloomy cemetery filled with weather-beaten wooden crosses as far as the eye could see.

'Dead from the last war,' someone muttered. 'Died in captivity in the stink-hole we're going to.'

They marched on. There was no let-up from the steady soaking drizzle. As dusk approached, they came in sight of Stalag VIIIb.

Germany's largest p.o.w. camp stood out in stark relief under the dun-coloured sky, and guard-dogs bayed in the distance. At the main gate the new arrivals were halted. After a long delay they were counted, then passed through a second wall of barbed wire fifteen feet high.

Warrant Officer Richard Pape was one of the most determined escapers of World War II. He found himself in the Hell Camp of Stalag VIIIb as punishment for evading capture.

Drenched to the skin, they had to be checked again before being marched into the RAF compound, a prison-within-a-prison comprising six long low barracks blocks. Finally, the men were dispersed to their allotted huts, shown to their bunks and given a meal.

First taste of Hell

On the following day, when they paraded for morning *appell*, they were able to see their new home and feel its bleakness. It was a vast army camp accommodating 20,000 British and Allied captives from Dunkirk and Crete. The RAF men were appalled at the obvious hatred with which the inmates of the camp were treated by their German guards. It was intense, potent and frightening, and it found expression in almost fanatical discipline. No wonder this place was called the 'Hell Camp'.

Just before the parade was dismissed, the German adjutant called out:

'Warrant Officer Pape. Step forward.'

One of the new arrivals stepped out of the ranks.

The officer gave a brusque order to a German NCO, who marched Pape to the Commandant's office. Then the parade was dismissed.

When Pape entered the Commandant's office, the German officer was reading a file. He ignored Pape for almost a minute before raising his eyes to look at him.

'I warn you, Pape,' he said in a soft thin voice. 'You step out of line once in this camp and I will send you to Strafe Lager.'

Pape said nothing. The Commandant spelled out the choices open to him. He could behave himself and make no attempt to escape; or he could be sent to the Reich's worst punishment camp for the duration of the war. The prisoner was dismissed.

He walked back to his hut, his mind clear on one thing. He would try to escape at the first opportunity.

His first thought centred around making a pair of wire-cutters. With so much barbed-wire surrounding the camp, this seemed to offer the most direct solution. But before he could get very far, another prisoner tried it and was shot to death beneath the inner fence. Pape looked around for alternatives.

Doubles all round

One day when he was idly watching a party of soldiers working in the compound erecting a new set of posts along one of the wire barricades, he noticed that one of the men looked not unlike himself, with almost the same figure, stature and colouring.

Maybe this offered a chance, he thought. Outside working parties always came from the Army. The RAF was never given the opportunity of getting outside the compound, and he, with his record, stood no chance, ever.

He waited a few days, then managed to mingle with the Army workers and to speak to the man who resembled him.

He was a New Zealander, Pape discovered. His name was Winston Yeatman. He was a Private from the 5th Field Company who had been captured in Crete.

Pape told Yeatman that he was planning to escape. He asked the New Zealander if he would consider changing identities with him, telling him the reasons.

Yeatman hestitated, and the RAF man went on, warning—

'It would be a hell of a risk you'd be taking. You'd be aiding and abetting a prisoner in an escape attempt. All I can promise you is that I would leave behind a document with our Camp Leader, in which I would try to take all the blame.'

They talked some more, and finally the New Zealander nodded with a grin.

'I'll do it,' he said.

Pape was astounded. 'Are you sure you wouldn't like to think about it?'

Dulag Luft **right**, *the first camp to hold Pape, was a transit camp. As soon as Pape had been identified as a trouble-maker and escaper he was destined for the journey to Stalag VIIIb, a top-security prison camp.*

'I've thought about it.'

Pape said: 'Thanks! I'll be in touch.'

His next step was to cultivate some of the Poles in the RAF compound. After a week or so of fraternizing, he chose a 26-year-old pilot named Mieteck to be his companion. Mieteck was lean and wiry, and as tough and taut as whipcord. He hated the Germans and Russians, and when he spoke of Poland there was a deep burning look in his smouldering eyes. Pape had him figured as a single-minded man who would be good to escape with. He took him aside one day and spoke to him.

Pape's plan was to find an exchange-identity for the Pole as well as for himself, enabling them both to cross over into the Army compound, where they would live until the opportunity came up to join an outside work detail. Then they would escape and cross the border into Poland, after which Mieteck would arrange shelter for them and ultimately assist Pape to get out of the country to Allied territory. Mieteck fervently agreed to join him.

Pape had been keeping a look-out for Yeatman, but hadn't managed to catch sight of him again. His only recourse was to go under the wire barricades and pay the New Zealander a visit in the Army compound, which was about 500 yards away. He needed to make a pair of wire-cutters, and had already worked out how.

He removed two flat strips of steel from the narrow edges of the fire-door in the wash-house. He bored a hole in the middle of both strips and fastened them together with a small nut and bolt. Then he sharpened the 'blades' with a file. They worked perfectly.

Pape's only hope of escape was to exchange identities—the German guards kept too tight a rein on this man they knew to be dangerous to miss any other attempt.
Top Private Winston Yeatman, a New Zealander, was the man Pape persuaded to change places.
Left A Pole, Mieteck Borodej, was Pape's running mate. He too exchanged identities with a New Zealander and when the break-out came would get clean away to carry on fighting the Germans.
Right The Allied authorities knew something was going on—but were not sure what.

The War Office,
Cas.P.W.
Curzon Street House
Curzon Street,
LONDON.W.1.
21st.September, 1942.

0103/4343.   Cas.(P.W.)

Madam,

I am directed to inform you that

No:937484 Sgt.R.B.P.PE, R.A.F.
and
No:32252 Pte.W.YEATMAN, N.Z.E.F.

both prisoners of war in Germany have apparently exchanged
identities without the knowledge of the German authorities.

This information may already have reached you and the
purpose of this communication is primarily to confirm that the
exchange has duly come to the knowledge of the authorities in the
United Kingdom.   The Department is unable to say for what precise
reason the exchange has been made although it is not thought that
there is any cause for uneasiness.

In the interests of both individuals it is important
that the enemy should not become aware of the exchange and you are
requested to write to Sgt:R.B.PAPE in the name of Pte: YEATMAN.
No enquiries by letter or otherwise should be made.

Quarterly parcels should be addressed in the same way
as letters and postcards.   To facilitate this the British Red Cross
Society, Prisoner of War Department, have been made aware of the
exchange of identity and they will ensure that no confusion arises.
in the packing centre.

If supplies of books. tobacco, etc., have been ordered
through permit holders you will no doubt wish to arrange for the
firms concerned to employ the altered form of address.

In matters of this kind the greatest discretion should
be observed and it is suggested that the facts should not be
discussed even among your friends.

Should you receive information that would lead you to
infer that the exchange of identity has been abandoned it would
be appreciated if this fact could be communicated to this Department
without delay.

I am, etc.
G.T.H.ROGERS.

To:-Mrs.Berry
etc.

77

Left Security in the Air Force section of Stalag VIIIb was so tight that Pape had first to break into the laxer Army compound before he could put his escape plan into operation. Here German guards search a fatigue party.

Above The men Pape left behind in Stalag VIIIb— but their work might have aided the escape.

Under the fence

One morning after roll call he went to the edge of the compound where several men were washing their clothes and stringing them up on wires to dry. Partly hidden by the washing, he cut a hole in the wire and wriggled under the fence on his belly to a deep drainage ditch running alongside the road 20 yards away. From here, he crawled along the ditch to a point level with the Army camp, cut a hole in the wire and wriggled through. He located Yeatman and told him about Mieteck and the need for another accomplice from within the Army compound. Yeatman said

he would see what could be arranged. Pape went back to his barracks by way of the ditch.

Three times during the next two weeks, Pape made this perilous journey to meet the New Zealander. There was a problem. Yeatman had spoken to some of his Army mates, some of whom he introduced to Pape. But none of them would agree to swap identities with a Pole. Too risky, they said. And try as they may, they couldn't find a running-mate for Yeatman. Disappointed, Pape returned to his compound.

He discussed the matter with Mieteck, who offered to put up money from his back pay to any soldier who would agree to swap identities with him.

However, before Pape could contact Yeatman again, something happened to put the Army compound out of reach for a while. A fellow-officer who was attempting to escape under the wire was shot dead. This was followed by a wave of vigilance and the introduction of stricter measures for deterring would-be escapers. Pape decided against a further sortie for the time being.

But a few days later a note reached him,

smuggled from the Army compound. It was from Yeatman, and it read:

'Dear Ginger. Have got a fellow-Kiwi to swop with the P. See you when convenient. W.Y.'

Mieteck was jubilant when Pape showed it to him.

A few days later, more than a hundred Russian prisoners arrived from Germany's eastern front. They were in appalling condition and teeming with body vermin. Before two days had passed, the whole camp was swarming with black typhus-carrying lice. The Russians, already weak from exposure and malnutrition, dropped like flies. Many of the other prisoners were affected, and the epidemic hit the surrounding villages, with the result that Stalag VIIIb was put under quarantine.

Each compound was segregated and closely guarded. Sentries were doubled. Medical orderlies arrived at the camp with portable de-lousers and fumigation equipment. The Commandant ordered all prisoners' heads to be shaved, and hair on every part of the body to be removed.

Pape saw his distinctive red locks disappear,

and his shorn skull was transformed to a glistening whiteness like those of all his mates. He decided that it was a stroke of good fortune. It would be so much easier for two bald-headed prisoners to swap identities.

Despite the risk, he decided that a move had to be made; so he crawled under the wire to see Yeatman and to meet his running-mate. It was another New Zealander. His name was George Potter. He told Pape that he was willing to swap identities with Mieteck. Relieved, Pape crawled back to his compound and told an equally grateful Mieteck.

Now Pape worked out the plan for the 'switch'. The mint tea kitchen was located in the centre of the camp, and every morning parties of four men,

Below Stalag VIIIb was exposed to the harsh climate of Central Europe.
Right For Pape, every activity linked with escape. In the camp pantomime, he is fourth from the left, he wore a wig that could be used to disguise himself as a woman for an escape attempt.

accompanied by an armed German guard, left the barracks of their respective compounds to collect a dustbin full of hot tea. This was obviously the place where the switch could be made. Pape and Mieteck would swap places with two of the rostered men from the RAF barracks; and Yeatman and Potter would swap with two Army men.

There was just one problem. The RAF detail was due to arrive at the tea kitchen at 0620, whereas the Army detail wouldn't get there until ten minutes later. Pape went under the wire again and discussed the plan with Yeatman and Potter, took their identity discs and gave them his own and Mieteck's. Then he returned to his compound for the final briefing with his Polish running-mate.

The switch

Dawn came. It was bitterly cold and snowing heavily. Pape and Mieteck were awakened unceremoniously by a German guard prodding them roughly in the back. They climbed out of bed and commenced to dress.

Pape had carefully hidden his trousers the night before, and now he couldn't find them. While the guard stood impatiently by, he went through the motions of looking for the missing garment, swearing about some 'stinking practical joker'. He found them after successfully delaying the RAF tea detail by four and a half minutes.

The four men struggled into their overcoats and tied scarves around their heads to stop their teeth from chattering. Then they stepped out on to the compound, followed by the German guard. He marched them briskly to the tea compound, carrying their empty dustbin between them. They arrived at the tea kitchen at 0627.

There was no sign of the Army detail. The German orderly placed the dustbin under the huge steel urn and turned on the cock to fill it three-quarters full with scalding tea. Time was running out, and Pape looked around the dark compound anxiously. The New Zealanders were nowhere in sight. Something had to be done.

At a nod from Pape, one of the squad members affected a dizzy spell and half-fell across the

dustbin, scalding his hand under the steaming stream of liquid. He let out a cry of pain and reeled away to the low stone wall nearby and began to vomit. It was an Academy Award performance, aided by the three other members of the detail, who stood by in an anxious group.

Some snow-shrouded figures emerged from across the compound and came to the tea kitchen. It was the Army detail. Yeatman and Potter made up the second row. Their dustbin was placed in position below the urn, the tap turned on. The four men stood huddled together close to the three members of the RAF detail.

The Army guard looked at the retching man and went across to exchange a few words with the RAF squad's guard. At that instant, the two New Zealanders changed places with Pape and Mieteck.

Presently, in response to a terse word from the guard, the sick prisoner recovered sufficiently to rejoin the squad, which, now struggling with the dustbinful of scalding tea, headed through the darkness towards the RAF compound. The switch had been made.

Into Poland

A few weeks later when the snow had cleared, the *Arbeits Offizier* called for four volunteers to work in a coalmine at Beuthen, just over the Polish border. Pape and Mieteck stepped forward. As there were no other volunteers, two men were picked at random to make up the detail—a huge Turkish soldier of fortune, and a

Pape could see little chance of escape direct from the Air Force section.
Top *Even the bleak buildings had been constructed with security in mind.*
Centre *The fatigue parties who worked outside the camp seemed to offer some hope—but they were drawn from the Army compound, not the Air Force. Pape's first move was to go under the wire—into the Army section.*
Left and right *Few men in Stalag VIIIb were as bent on escape as Richard Pape—but while they settled down to last out the war, he schemed.*

small wiry Greek. On the following morning they were marched under an armed guard out of the camp to the railway station at Annaberg, where they caught the train into Poland.

During the first few weeks in the coalmine, it seemed as though they had come from the frying pan into the fire. Working long hours in a briquette factory, they had to contend with harsh discipline and unrelenting pressure from the brutal German guards.

But as the days passed, they systematically smuggled their escape supplies into the bath-house and hid them behind a row of lockers.

Pape's escape plan was simple. Each shift of labourers had to march to the bath house, where they changed into underground apparel and re-assembled in the doorway for counting. The guards then marched them to the platform cage where the military guards handed them over to the civilian overseers. Here, there was a further count as the prisoners entered the cages.

Pape had worked out that the critical time-slot for the escape was the ten-minute interval between the pit-head counts.

The morning finally came, and when they arrived at the bath house they put on their pit clothes over their escape suits, collected their supplies from behind the lockers and took their positions in the squad.

The guards counted the prisoners then gave the command to march.

The small column of men crunched along the gravel road. There was snow falling lightly now, and visibility was poor. Presently the black bulk of piled pit machinery loomed ahead, and they were in a narrow no-man's land between heaven and hell.

Only 70 yards to go.

Making the break

Suddenly, the front two prisoners turned on each other in well-rehearsed argument. They began to wrestle and curse each other. The German guards rushed forward to break them apart.

In that instant, Pape threw himself down beside a stack of wood. A second later, Mieteck joined him. They lay still as the rest of the party marched on to the pit head. The two men were still arguing.

Pape and Mieteck got up and ran 40 feet to a narrow bridge which spanned an 80-foot cutting. The bridge was guarded by a huge steel door which was locked, and on either side by a high steel fence, from which were stretched strands of barbed wire to about ten feet along the parapet.

Mieteck reached the bridge first. He gripped the barbed wire with his leather-faced mittens and flung himself outwards over the 40-foot drop, and hauled himself hand-over-hand to the parapet. Pape followed, also wearing leather mittens. His heavy weight loosened the wire and it sagged down dangerously. He was swinging below the bridge, and other strands of barbed wire became hooked to his clothes.

Behind him, a whistle blew, and there were shouts from the German guards. A second later, the beam of a searchlight cut through the gloom from the main tower. And there was Pape spread-eagled on the strands halfway across the parapet.

Mieteck leaned down and grabbed him, pulled him up, as footsteps reached the other side of the door.

The two men bent double and ran across the 80 feet of wooden sleepers as the beam of the searchlight followed them and the guards opened fire with submachine guns.

They reached the end and took the metal steps leading down two at a time, as bullets zinged past their ears and ripped into the super-structure.

From the Army compound Pape's next move was to volunteer for the even harsher conditions of work in a coalmine across the Polish border—K stands for knappe or miner. He and Mieteck hoped a chance for escape would soon come.

A guard was suddenly in front of them. Before he could bring his rifle up to fire, Pape caught him in the crutch with his boot and he fell away with a sobbing cry.

They came down to ground level, reached the railway lines, found the shelter of the coal trucks, scrambled over some squalid sidings, and reached the field.

They crossed it, ankle deep in snow, almost a quarter of a mile. They reached the perimeter of the mine, which was surrounded by a wire mesh fence 15 feet high.

As they neared it, Pape reached over his shoulder for a metal hook and rope which he had assembled to overcome this barrier. It was not there. He had left it behind in the bath house!

Mieteck ran up and down beside the fence. He ran out of sight. Pape, cursing at his own stupidity, and gulping in lungfuls of ice-cold air, stood crouched and defeated.

Then he heard a voice. The Pole was calling desperately to him. He turned and staggered through the falling snow. He saw Mieteck on his knees beside the fence, digging the earth furiously with his knife.

'Dig!' he gasped. 'Dig!'

Pape went down on his knees beside him. At the base of the fence was a five-inch clearance. The two men feverishly scraped out the rocky earth beneath it. They worked like crazy men to enlarge the opening, then wriggled under the wire one at a time.

They ran away from the compound and took shelter in a valley long enough to remove their pit clothes. Then they turned east towards the holy city of Czestochowa.

They had made it.

Below This sequence shows how prisoners could make a simple compass from items readily available or 'procurable' in a prison camp plus aids concealed in the parcels the German authorities allowed through to the prisoners.
Richard Pape gave as well as receiving. Throughout his captivity he sent coded messages back to Britain about troop movements, bomb damage and other military information. Some of these messages he hid in the hollowed-out heads of finger rings shaped from toothbrush handles. These hollow rings had another purpose, too—carrying poison to use against traitors and squealers.

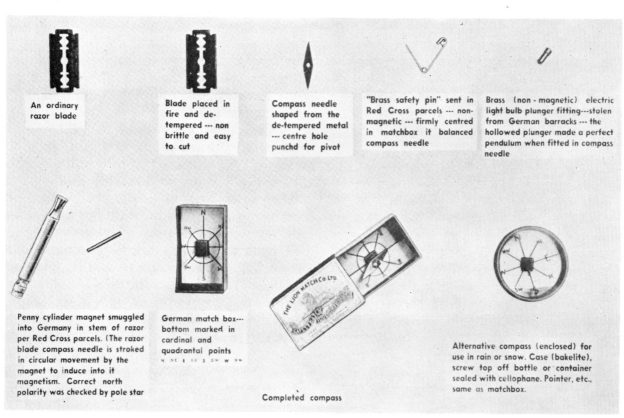

An ordinary razor blade

Blade placed in fire and de-tempered --- non brittle and easy to cut

Compass needle shaped from the de-tempered metal --- centre hole punchd for pivot

"Brass safety pin" sent in Red Cross parcels --- non-magnetic --- firmly centred in matchbox it balanced compass needle

Brass (non-magnetic) electric light bulb plunger fitting---stolen from German barracks --- the hollowed plunger made a perfect pendulum when fitted in compass needle

Penny cylinder magnet smuggled into Germany in stem of razor per Red Cross parcels. (The razor blade compass needle is stroked in circular movement by the magnet to induce into it magnetism. Correct north polarity was checked by pole star

German match box--- bottom marked in cardinal and quadrantal points N NE E SE S SW W NW

Completed compass

Alternative compass (enclosed) for use in rain or snow. Case (bakelite), screw top off bottle or container sealed with cellophane. Pointer, etc., same as matchbox.

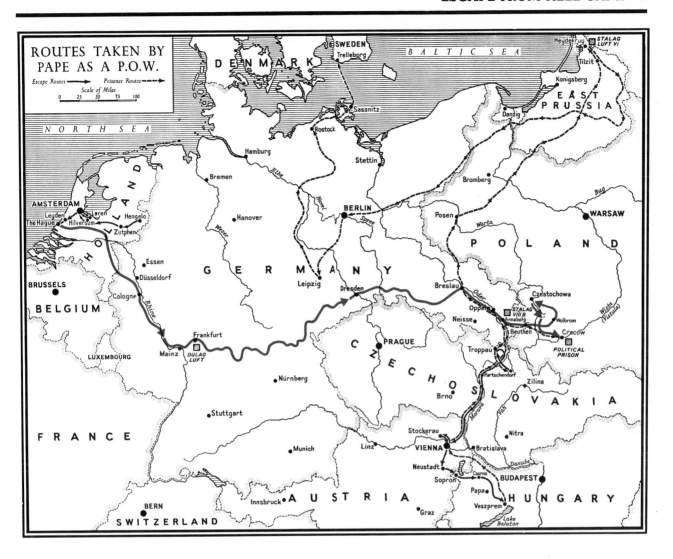

ROUTES TAKEN BY PAPE AS A P.O.W.

Escape Routes ⟶   Prisoner Routes ⟶

Scale of Miles
0   25   50   75   100

Richard Pape's break-out from Hell Camp failed—but he did eventually suceed in getting back to Britain after his 'travels' as prisoner and escaper.

After being sheltered by the Sisters of Mercy in Czestochowa, the two men caught a train to Cracow, where Pape, ill with pleurisy, was recaptured by the Gestapo and tortured. Mieteck managed to escape and carried on fighting the Germans.

Pape was taken to Troppou, in Czechoslovakia, to a German-controlled prison-farm. After sabotaging equipment, he escaped again, only to be caught once more. He found himself back in Stalag VIIIb—as Yeatman. After identities had been straightened out he **was taken to Luft VI, on the Lithuanian border.**

Here, by means of an ingenious scheme involving a hollowed-out wooden penis filled with another prisoner's nephritis-laden urine, he was able to fool the German doctors into believing that he was suffering from kidney disease, and was passed for repatriation. He and several other prisoners were put aboard the German vessel Deutschland bound for Trelleborg in Sweden and freedom. Pape arrived there on September 7, 1944—exactly three years since he had been shot down. After being fed and feted for a week in Sweden, he boarded the Gripsholm, arriving in Liverpool, England, six days later.

THE WOODEN HORSE

Dig a hole in the middle of the compound—when the huts are so far from the perimeter wire that is the only way to build an escape tunnel. For the seasoned escapers of Stalag Luft III hope lay in a vaulting horse—the wooden horse—that kept the Germans amused while men inside burrowed their way out.

It was January 1943 when Flight Lieutenant Eric Williams and Captain Michael Codner came to **Stalag Luft III**, to find the compound a depressing sea of mud and the Silesian countryside bleak and snow-covered.

Both men had escaped from their previous camp, only to be arrested in Poland and brought to **Stalag Luft III**, where they were quite happy to remain while the weather was so bitter. But after the snow had melted and gone and spring came to Sagan, their thoughts turned once again to finding a means of escape.

During the previous few months at **Stalag Luft III**, all the escape tunnels being constructed beneath the prison camp by its inmates had been discovered. The German ferrets were becoming expert at locating them, constantly crawling under the huts, listening for the scrape of a spade, and searching for tell-tale deposits of yellow earth.

It was Eric Williams who first decided that tunnelling from the huts had finally become an obsolete method of escape. Too far from the perimeter, he told his friend Michael Codner. Too long to build it. You were ninety-nine per cent certain of being discovered. What was needed was a way of making the tunnel shorter, and of starting it well away from the huts. From this discussion came Williams' idea of the wooden horse.

Left The Wooden Horse seemed innocuous to the Germans—just a vaulting box made of Red Cross chests—but it meant freedom for three men.
Below One of the three was Flight Lieutenant Oliver Philpot, here, third from left, in Stalag Luft III with crew members of his shot down plane.

Codner didn't think he was serious.

'A Trojan Horse?'

No, not a battering ram, Williams explained. A vaulting horse with a padded top and sloping sides, like they used to vault over in the school

Once the vaulting team had gone through their routine for a week, establishing the Wooden Horse as a natural part of the compound's scenery in the eyes of the guards, Eric 'Bill' Williams, the man who thought of the idea, concealed himself in the box while it was carried out and then began burrowing through the soil.

The men of the vaulting team were almost as heroic as the escapers themselves—making a two-hour session look natural was no easy task—and it was because of his willingness to organize this soul-destroying task that the third member of the team, Oliver Philpot, was recruited.

gymnasium. Yes, they would get together a team of physical-fitness enthusiasts and hold afternoon sessions, vaulting over it. And while this was going on, someone would be inside the horse, digging the shaft of an escape tunnel.

They put their idea up to the Escape Committee. They were all for it, and gave it their enthusiastic backing. Williams and Codner set to work constructing their wooden horse.

It stood four feet six inches high, with sloping sides giving it a base of five feet long by three feet wide. The frame was built of sturdy timber. The sides and ends were made from plywood panels taken from tea-chests sent from the Red Cross. The top was made of solid boards which were padded with bedding and covered with calico. The tools and materials used were either stolen or 'borrowed' from inside the camp.

Gymnastics

The double doors of the canteen swung open and a group of prisoners dressed in shorts and sand-shoes burst out and run across to the far side of the compound. Behind them came four men, similarly clad, carrying a wooden vaulting horse on two poles. They carried it to a spot about ten yards from the trip-wire that ran along inside the perimeter fence.

As soon as the horse had been placed in position, the poles were slipped out of the holes in the side of the structure and the gymnasium instructor took over. He formed the prisoners up in single file, spoke to them briefly, then led the way over the horse with a simple leap-frogging vault. One by one the men followed.

Alerted that something unusual was happening, the German guards in the towers looked down into the compound with curiosity and suspicion. They had learned to regard any unfamiliar happening in the prison camp with distrust, for often in the past they had been put on by the prisoners with the express purpose of diverting the attention of the guards while some other event—more often than not connected with an escape-attempt—was taking place somewhere else in the camp. A boxing match had been used more than once.

91

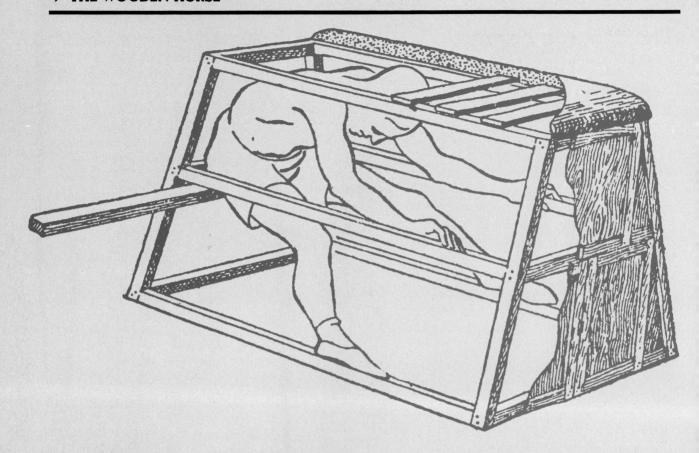

The guards watched the vaulting prisoners; but also they kept their eyes on the rest of the camp, and particularly the barbed-wire barricade surrounding it. After a time, the Camp Commandant came out to take a long look at what was going on in the compound; then he went back to his office, apparently satisfied.

The strenuous activity went on, the men obviously enjoying it. The instructor altered the jump. The men tried it. Some got over skilfully. Others didn't make it. By now, many of the other prisoners had gathered around to watch and barrack. One of the prisoners was awkward and below standard. His run-up amused the crowd and drew a cheer each time it was his turn. The German guards watched with amusement, grateful for something to take their minds off their boredom.

Now the men were taken to a different position, so that they could approach the horse from the side. The instructor ran up and executed a simple two-handed straddle. The men followed. When it came to the camp 'character's' turn, he missed his footing and ran smack into the horse, knocking it over. It went on its side, its empty

Above The vaulters carried out a single man concealed in the box. On the first day he lifted 12 bags of sand and constructed a hatch that hid the tell-tale hole in the compound.
Right In this way they dug 40 feet in two months—with 70 feet still to go they changed the system so that two men could work in the tunnel at once.

interior being in full view of the guards. After the laughing had stopped, the instructor had the men hoist it back in position, and the vaulting exercises continued.

It went on for two hours. By this time the novelty of the spectacle had worn off, and the guards gave the gymnasts only a desultory glance from time to time. Finally, the instructor called it a day, and the men carried the horse back to the canteen.

Before they left the canteen, one of the men tied a thread of black cotton across the doorway. On the following morning, they found that the thread had been broken. The horse had been examined by the Germans during the night.

The digging begins

The vaulters repeated their routine every day for a week, during which time the horse was knocked over many times.

One bright afternoon, the structure was carried out as usual and set up. The instructor went over first, and the men followed. The procedure went on as on previous occasions. But this time, the men had been warned against knocking over the horse. There was a man inside it, already scooping up the dark grey sand from the surface of the earth and putting it into a cardboard box.

On the first day when Williams hid inside the horse, as soon as the vaulting had started, he scraped up the dark grey surface sand and put it into a cardboard box. Then, with a bricklayer's trowel, he started to dig the shaft, scooping out the bright yellow sand and putting it into cloth bags made from trouser-legs. As he filled each bag, he hung it from a hook in the roof of the horse.

It was very hot inside the cramped enclosed space, and soon he was drenched with perspiration. He had to work hard on this first day in order to establish an entrance to the shaft

which could be covered securely before the vaulting session finished. He had brought with him inside the horse one of the Red Cross tea-chests, from which the lid and bottom panel had been removed. This was used as the shoring for the sides of the shaft. Having sunk the hollow box, with the top edges six inches below the surface, he placed the lid on top, covered it with earth, which he rammed down tight, then sprinkled it with the dark grey surface sand from the cardboard box. Then he knocked gently to tell Michael Codner that he was ready to leave.

The vaulters stopped, pushed the poles through the holes and carried the horse—now heavy with not only Williams' weight but 12 bags of sand—back to the canteen. Here, they lifted it up for Williams to get out, and transferred the sand into long sausage-like bags which the men tied to their belts and strung inside their trousers for later dispersal around the camp.

The incredible venture went on. The two men took it in turns to go down. They made the entrance shaft five feet deep and placed the plywood box on four stacks of bricks, shored up on three sides. They now dug horizontally, and shored up the walls and roof of the tunnel with ready-cut bed-boards removed from the bunks. The digger had to work lying on his back,

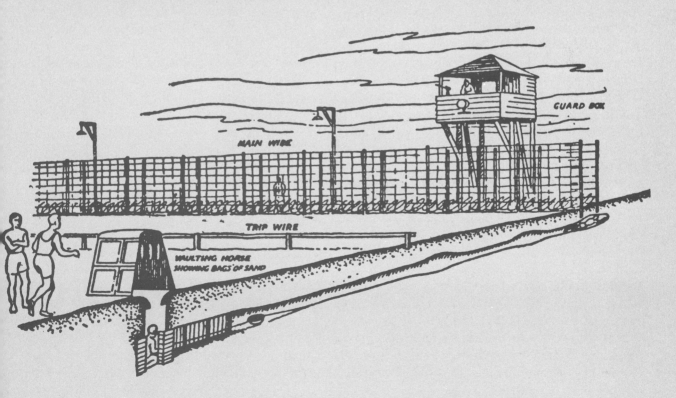

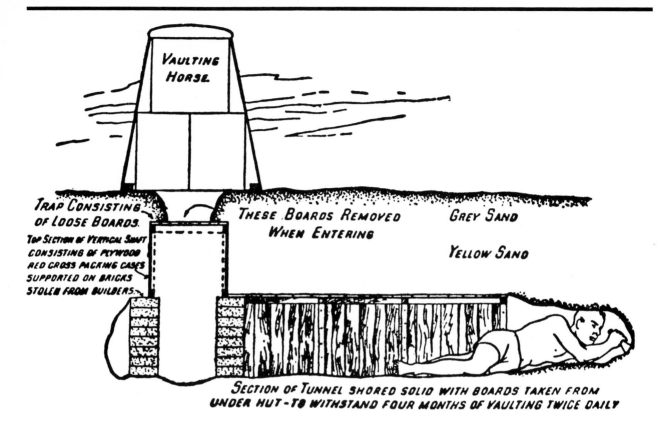

VAULTING HORSE.

TRAP CONSISTING OF LOOSE BOARDS.

TOP SECTION OF VERTICAL SHAFT CONSISTING OF PLYWOOD RED CROSS PACKING CASES SUPPORTED ON BRICKS STOLEN FROM BUILDERS.

THESE BOARDS REMOVED WHEN ENTERING

GREY SAND

YELLOW SAND

SECTION OF TUNNEL SHORED SOLID WITH BOARDS TAKEN FROM UNDER HUT - TO WITHSTAND FOUR MONTHS OF VAULTING TWICE DAILY

The shored-up section of the tunnel stood up to the thump of the vaulters' feet—but disaster almost struck when another section caved in. Quick action by a vaulter who collapsed across the hole with a 'broken leg' saved the day.

scraping away the sand, then jamming the bearers into position before inserting the bed-boards.

The tunnel grew as the days and weeks went by. They shored up 20 feet, after which they pressed forward towards the perimeter without any supports. The work had become very difficult and fatiguing. The air in the tunnel was foul, but they couldn't put air holes up yet for fear of discovery by guard dogs. It took two months to dig forty feet.

Cave in

One afternoon the tunnel caved in. To cover the hole, one of the vaulters, Nigel Wilde, fell across it, pretending to have broken his leg.

Codner was inside, and Williams, who had gone to the canteen to get something, came hurrying back when he saw that the vaulters had stopped.

'What's the matter?' he asked anxiously.

'Tunnel's caved in', one of the men told him.

'Get a stretcher', Williams said. 'And don't panic.'

Two men hurried off to the hospital ward.

Williams crouched near Wilde and the other prisoners crowded around them. Williams thrust his arm down into the loose sand and cleared a hole to the tunnel.

'Mike!' he called softly.

'Hullo', a voice came up through the opening.

'Are you alright?'

'Yes. I'm trying to shore it up. Can you fill in the hole?'

'Yes.'

The men came back with the stretcher and a first aid kit. Wilde was placed on it, and Williams made a big show of binding the injured man's leg while the other vaulters levelled out the hollow as best they could, and covered the depression with grey sand.

Ten minutes went by, and the men became aware that the German guards were more than interested in the proceedings, and that at any moment one of them would advise the Commandant that something unusual was going on. But finally Codner came up into the horse and closed over the entrance to the shaft. They carried the horse back to the canteen, and others carried Wilde to his barracks.

A few days later, both Codner and Williams collapsed from exhaustion and were all for abandoning the project. In all this time they had only completed 40 feet out of a total of 110. Seventy more feet to go. They were both ready to admit that they had bitten off more than they could chew. The main trouble, they both agreed, was the lack of air, and no light. And the one-man operation down in the tunnel was far too slow.

'Maybe we should *both* go down', Codner suggested.

'But it's all the chaps can do to carry the horse and *one* man, let alone two—plus a double supply of sand!'

Williams refused to be deterred. In the first session, he said, they'd both go down the shaft, at the bottom of which they would build a work chamber. They would fill 36 bags of sand and stack them in the shaft, close it up and both go back in the horse. In the next session, *one* of them would go back, pick up 12 bags of sand, and come back. In the third session, the other man would do the same; and in the fourth session, the first man would go down and get the remaining 12 bags and come back with them. Then they would start the routine again.

All this time, the gymnasts had stalwartly carried on with their daily vaulting stint. But there were signs that without a leader enthusiasm was waning. It was plain that they

For the final break-out, Codner sweated out a long wait in the tunnel until the vaulters could bring out Williams and Philpot, in black combinations, to join him. The third man in the box was McKay, a New Zealander whose job was to close the shaft behind the three escapers.

would have to bring someone else in on the escape. They approached Flight Lieutenant Oliver Philpot, and he agreed to organize and conduct the vaulting programme.

Past the wire

The pleasant Silesian summer was drawing to a close by the time Williams and Codner had pushed the tunnel under the wire barricade; and now the vaulting sessions were becoming fewer. There had been numerous alarums and excursions, including several narrow escapes and moments of tension as tempers frayed. But the time came at last to check the length of the tunnel.

Williams went down one afternoon with a poker. He crawled to the end of the tunnel and pushed the end of the poker up through the sand until it broke surface. A vaulter, who was straddling the horse, saw the thin piece of metal emerge about three feet beyond the wire—and about 15 feet left of where it was supposed to be.

That evening they discussed the pros and cons of the situation. The only railway time-table in the camp would expire in a week's time, so the three men were determined to make the break as soon as possible. With the hole only three feet beyond the barbed-wire barricade, they would have to do some more digging to make the tunnel longer. There was a ditch only nine feet further on, into which the searchlight threw a shadow. This became their objective.

On September 28 they had pushed the tunnel as far as they dare, and dug a bulge to hold their kitbags and escape gear. They were ready to make the break. Williams and Codner went down during the early afternoon vaulting session. Codner crawled to the end bulge and made an air-hole to sweat out the long wait. Williams came back up, closed the shaft and was taken back to the canteen.

At the afternoon *appell*, the Senior British Officer wore Codner's uniform and took his

The three escapers had made every preparation: train times, routes, they knew the lot. This is Oliver Philpot's home-made compass.

The Allied escape machine provided maps of potential escape routes printed on silk or rustle-free paper that could be folded small enough to defy a German search.

place. And immediately afterwards the vaulters assembled at the canteen. Williams and Philpot, completely covered in black combinations, positioned themselves inside the horse. Between their knees, they held a New Zealander named McKay. The two poles were shoved through and the gymnasts carried the creaking horse across the compound, set it down and began the session.

Williams and Philpot went down and made contact with Codner to see if he was alright. Then McKay closed the shaft and waited in the horse, to be carried at the close of the day's vaulting.

This was the danger period for the three men in the tunnel. Fully clothed, plus their black combinations, they had to wait in a space 25 feet long and two feet square, that was ventilated by one small hole three inches in diameter. Working with a torch, they pushed through the last few feet towards the ditch without benefit of shoring. If the tunnel should collapse now they would be buried alive.

Breakout

Darkness fell over the camp, and back in the barracks men were blowing trumpets and

and walked towards the centre of the forest, then to the railway station only a mile away, and the promise of a journey to the coast, and after that to freedom . . .

Once inside the forest, Williams and Codner stripped off their black combination suits, washed each other's faces with their hand-kerchiefs, put on civilian hats and mackintoshes, and headed for the railway station. They were lucky. A train had just pulled in, and they boarded it. It took them to Frankfurt, from where they caught a train to Kustrin, and from Kustrin to Stettin.

Here for some days, they passed themselves off as Frenchmen and put up at the Hotel

Left Oliver Philpot later restaged some aspects of his successful escape for the press. Here he re-enacts an attempt to smuggle himself aboard a neutral Swedish ship.
Right. The papers they had prepared in Stalag Luft III, this is Oliver Philpot's false identification as a Swede, stood up to scrutiny by police, railway clerks, hotel keepers, dock guards . . .
While still in camp they had decided that the best way of moving through war-time Germany was to travel openly.

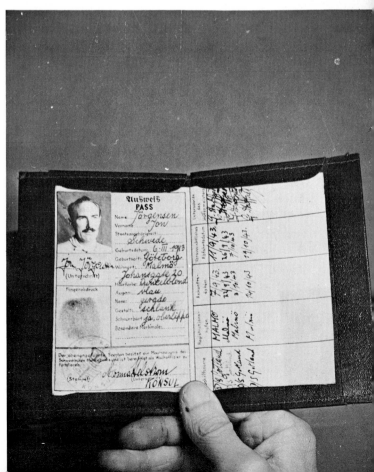

singing. The noise wafted to the diggers when Codner broke the surface of the ditch and he saw the black sky and the glint of early evening stars.

He pushed his kitbag ahead of him into the ditch and crawled through after it. Williams wriggled out after him, and then lay in the ditch. Further along the tunnel, Philpot was following.

For a few seconds, they lay there listening. The compound was as bright as day under the floodlights. The party in the huts sounded more boisterous than ever. Codner picked up his kitbag and ran into the pine forest. Williams followed him. From the shadows of the trees, they could see no sign of Philpot. They turned

Schobel. They haunted the Freihaven docks looking for a Swedish ship, but after a narrow escape decided on a different course. Through an English-speaking French barber they were able to get inside a French labour camp, and to meet a man named René who had contacts with the Danish underground. At last they were taken on board a Danish cargo ship, the *S I Jacobsen*, bound for Copenhagen, and placed in the charge of a man named Sigmund, a member of the Danish Underground.

To Denmark...

During the voyage, the captain received a warning that the German SS were waiting at Copenhagen to arrest Sigmund, and that the Underground had arranged for a small boat to rendezvous with the ship before it reached port. As day dawned the following morning Sigmund, Williams and Codner were taken ashore in the small boat as German patrol vessels were heading for the Danish ship. The three men were provided with bicycles on which they sped to an isolated farmhouse which was the district head-quarters of the Underground. A few days later, Sigmund took them into Copenhagen and hid them at his sister's flat until the *S I Jacobsen* was ready to leave.

On the afternoon they were to leave, Sigmund went down to the docks to arrange for their embarkation. He returned with the news that the Jerries were swarming all over the docks. He took them into town and bought tickets for the electric railway. As darkness came they headed out into the Danish countryside.

They left the train at a small wayside station, and Sigmund led them to a bridge. It was a long walk, and as they approached it, their footsteps were deadened by fallen leaves. There was now bright moonlight, and the steel bridge looked naked and without cover.

Sigmund warned that there was a guard on the bridge and that there were other guards on the island. Codner pretended he was wounded and staggered out into the open. The sentry challenged:

'Halt ! Wer ist dort?'

Codner groaned and sank to his knees. The German went cautiously towards him with his rifle, bayonet fixed, at the ready. He stopped to look at the moaning stranger.

...a killing...

Williams chose that moment to attack the sentry from behind with a sock full of sand, while Codner threw himself at the man's knees. In the scuffle that followed Codner was knocked unconscious with the butt of the German's rifle—but Williams killed the sentry by choking him.

...and freedom

Meanwhile, Sigmund had crossed the river to steal a boat. He was ready for them. They waded into the shallow water and helped him heave the boat into deep water. They clambered aboard and the two Englishmen hoisted the sail while Sigmund steered, tacking along the shore-line in the light off-shore wind. They would be in Sweden by the morning.

Two days later —on October 29, 1943 — Williams and Codner were sitting in the office of the British Consul at Goteborg. They asked after Oliver Philpot and were told that he had arrived a week before and was still in Goteborg. That evening the three of them met and celebrated, and Philpot told them how he had got a train to Danzig and stowed away on a Swedish ship the same night, landing him at Goteborg.

Three days later they were flown to England.

The three escapers split up after breaking out: Oliver Philpot (centre) made a blitz up to Danzig and across to Sweden; but the other two, Codner (left) and Williams were only nine days behind and here are reunited in a Swedish hotel.

RENDEZVOUS 127

Bravery and cheek brought success to Madame Brusselmans, an important link in the Comète Line, a Belgian underground organization rescuing Allied servicemen trapped in occupied territory, as she risked her life to bring two Americans to safety. If the Gestapo found them, Anne Brusselmans would die.

AVIS

L'AUTORITE MILITAIRE ALLEMANDE NOUS COMMUNIQUE CE QUI SUIT :
CONDAMNATIONS A MORT

Les citoyens belges Eric de Menten de Horne, Jean Ingels, Emile Delbruyère, Albert Marchal, Henri Rasquin, Ghislain Neybergh, Gaston Biainsi que les ressortissants français Edouard Verpraet et Antoine Renaud ont été condamnés à mort par un tribunal de guerre pour activité en faveur de l'ennemi.

Le jugement a été exécuté par fusillade.

Une partie des condamnés agissant comme membres d'une organisation constituée à cet effet, les autres n'ayant aucun rapport avec elle, ont soustrait des aviateurs ennemis abattus à l'arrestation de la part de l'autorité occupante, les ont pourvus de vêtements civils, Lébergés et ont aidé leur fuite d'une façon quelconque. Dans cet ordre d'idées, il y a lieu de souligner à nouveau que les tribunaux militaires appliqueront impitoyablement à l'avenir également en cas d'appui donné à des membres d'armées ennemies, les peines les plus sévères prévues par la loi. En conséquence, quiconque vient en aide de n'importe quelle façon à un aviateur ennemi, quiconque omet de signaler des membres d'armées ennemies au poste allemand le plus proche, doit se rendre compte des conséquences de son acte et ne peut compter sur aucune indulgence de la part des tribunaux.

AGE DE DOCUMENTS FALSIFIES.

They were nine hours in the water before a member of the Belgian underground came and found them.

Their saviour was the young son of a local farmer. He arrived in a rowboat and helped them to a hiding place, then ran off to bring back a doctor and a nurse who gave Marty morphia and attended to his burns. Then they were taken to the nearby farm.

Several days later, they were brought into Brussels by the Belgian underground, and housed in an apartment owned by 'Mr P'.

It was September 10, 1943. A light rain had been falling all day, and the Rue d'Ixelles, its surface wet and glistening, was dark and deserted. After 9 p.m. the curfew kept Brussels' streets clear of people, many of them were huddled safely in their homes surreptitiously listening to the BBC.

Left Execution by firing squad—that was the risk Anne Brusselmans ran when she helped American fliers Hank Sarnow and Marty Minnick.
Above Marty Minnick from Ohio was seriously burned when his uniform caught fire before he could bale out of the flaming plane.
Right Hank Sarnow, here in Anne Brusselmen's apartment, dragged him to shelter.

On September 2, 1943, a USAF Flying Fortress returning from a daylight raid on Berlin was hit and set on fire over Maastrich, Belgium, and its crew baled out. One of the men, Marty Minnick, from Ohio, jumped out with his uniform on fire, and by the time he had hit the ground was severely burned. Fortunately he landed near a river, and another crew member, 'Hank' Sarnow, from Chicago, dragged him into the water and sheltered him among the bulrushes.

They had to stay in the water until dark because the Germans had seen the crew bale out and were strenuously searching the countryside for them.

Can you take two puppies?

From a darkened balcony on the second floor of the gas company building (Number 127), Madame Brusselmans watched the dark sky and listened for Allied bombers, but the night was still. It was part of her job to pin-point searchlight and ack-ack batteries and to send reports through the underground pipeline back to England.

Just after half-past nine the phone rang. She hurried into the flat and answered it.

'Hullo.'

'Can you take two puppies?' a female voice asked, in French. Madame Brusselmans recognized the voice of Michou.

'When?' she asked.

'At once.'

'Does it have to be tonight?'

'Yes.' Michou kept her voice even. 'The mother is ill—and one of the puppies—', her voice faltered, '—has a bad paw.'

'I see.'

'You don't mind?'

'Of course not. I'll come and get them.'

Madame Brusselmans put down the phone. Michou's call had told her that two Allied airmen in her care had to be moved urgently because the person who was sheltering them was in danger of being arrested by the Gestapo; and one of the airmen was injured.

She went into the bedroom, put on her coat and hat, peeped at her two sleeping children, then let herself out of the flat and went along the dark corridor to the elevator. She took it to the ground floor and a few seconds later unlocked the door and stepped out into the Rue d'Ixelles. She turned left and hurried along the pavement in the fine drenching rain.

Just over three years ago, Anne Brusselmans and her husband Julien had started helping Allied soldiers and airmen who were on the run from the Germans in Belgium. At first they gave supplies of clothes and food to a Protestant padre, who passed them on to the underground escape organisation. Then, at the padre's request, she translated the BBC News into French for distribution to Belgian patriots in order to keep up their spirits of resistance.

By July, 1941, RAF bombers were attacking the Reich almost nightly, and Allied air crews were being shot down over Belgium in growing numbers. One day a friend of the Brusselmans brought a retired Belgian Army officer to meet them. After asking several questions, he told them he was looking for a suitable house in which to shelter some of the airmen.

When they appeared to hesitate, he pointed out that 127 Rue d'Ixelles was ideal. It was surrounded by balconies and had five exits, plus a fire-escape. It was ideal for a quick getaway in case the building should be searched.

The Brusselmans hesitated. It was one thing to provide food and clothes and make translations of BBC broadcasts. But this was something different. This was direct participation in aiding Germany's enemies to escape. They eventually agreed.

The Comète line

They did not know it then, but they had just become an important link in what was to become an underground French-Belgian escape organization which was later to become known as the Comète Line.

From then on, there was a steady stream of airmen through the Brusselmans' flat—British, Australians, Canadians, New Zealanders and—after Pearl Harbour—Americans.

The Comète Line was to guide to safety through German-occupied territory over a thousand men—enough to provide crews for several fighter wings, or one complete bomber group. These men brought back vital information about conditions in occupied Europe—data about potential targets for air attack and about the morale of both the Germans and the resistance groups.

When Anne arrived at 'Mr P's' house and

Anne Brusselmans' apartment on the second floor of 127 Rue d'Ixelles, Brussels (marked by arrow) was a clearing house for the Comète line, the Belgian underground organization that helped Allied servicemen evade the Germans.

found that one of the Americans could scarcely walk, she decided that it would be too dangerous to attempt to cross the city with them during the curfew. She brought Hank back to her flat alone.

On the following morning she took him down town, where they picked up Marty and went to a photographer's to have the pictures taken for their new French identity cards. On the way home they boarded a tram.

It was a risky thing to do, but with Marty's injured leg to consider, Anne had no choice. The Germans had started stopping trams at random and searching civilians. They made them get off and stand facing the walls with their hands above their heads while the Germans searched them and checked their identity papers. Fortunately, there was no such check this morning.

A Lucky Strike could kill

A German soldier was standing close to them, his thumbs hooked in his pistol belt. He glanced at the three of them indifferently as the tram lurched forward. Hank looked studiously at the window facing him, and Marty fumbled in the pockets of his jacket and produced a pack of cigarettes. The German had fixed his attention on Anne. She stiffened as out of the corner of her eye she saw Marty draw out a cigarette, crumple the pack and toss it towards the open window. It struck the frame and fell at the feet of the German soldier.

For several blocks, Anne was aware of the German's eyes on her face. Once, when he looked away, she fleetingly glanced down at the wad of paper and cellophane. She could read the English words: *Lucky Strike*, etched in bold black on a crimson circle.

The tram slowed to a stop.

She said brightly: 'Come.'

She took Marty's arm and helped him off the tram. Hank followed them.

As soon as they were safely inside her flat she told them:

'That cigarette could have cost us our lives.'

Marty was profuse in his apologies, particularly when he realized that his unconscious

The Gestapo were always active—searching trams was a favourite ploy. Because of Marty's injuries the escapers decided to risk a tram journey. Then Marty, standing beside a German soldier, lit up a Lucky Strike—an American cigarette . . .

and seemingly harmless act in lighting a cigarette could have been enough to betray all three of them to the Gestapo.

With evaders hiding in their apartment almost constantly, the Brusselmans family lived through day-to-day tensions which would have terrified the average citizen. Their six-year-old son Jacques kept watch in the corridor, and every time the lift came up he ran to the sitting room to close the door. He didn't know who the strangers were, but he sensed the danger and knew that they must not be seen by friends or visitors.

Julien Brusselman's job as an official of the gas company was an advantage, as he could see everything that went on at street level.

The Gestapo are here

One morning, when Anne had just given breakfast to the two Americans, the telephone rang. She answered it.

'Anne?'

She recognized her husband's voice.

'Yes.'

'The Gestapo are here.'

'What?'

'Tell the boys to stay put.'

Click. The phone went silent.

Anne dialled several numbers, ringing other offices in the building, to warn people she knew to be secret members of the Belgian Army. Then she went in to see the Americans.

'The Gestapo are here. Get dressed and stay in this room. Don't move or make a sound until I come and tell you what to do.'

She left them and closed the door. Then she went out and stationed herself on the balcony and looked down into the Rue d'Ixelles.

Several police and Army vehicles were parked in front of the entrance and groups of SS men

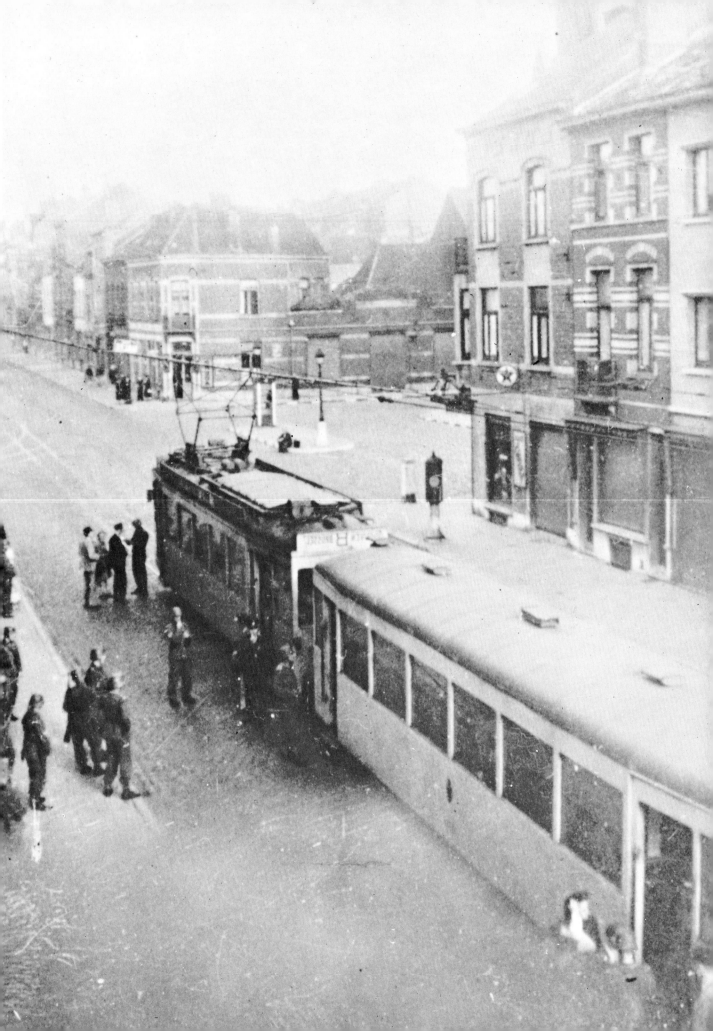

were stationed on the pavement. Presently a young man she knew as 'Robert' was brought out at the point of a pistol. Behind him came two Gestapo officers carrying piles of papers and books which they had taken from his office.

Anne looked down helplessly. There was nothing she could do. And there was nothing that her husband and the other men in the offices could do, even though they outnumbered the Germans, who were heavily armed, and who could bring in reinforcements at the slightest signal of resistance.

Robert was shoved into a car and driven off. Anne found out later that he had been arrested for intelligence activities and condemned to death.

All was clear again. The official cars drove off and the entrance was cleared of the SS men. She went into the flat and told the Americans to relax.

There was much to do to prepare them for the next stage of their journey back to England. She dressed them both as French civilians, with brand new Austrian overcoats. They had no French to speak of, and she got them to repeat their French names and the supposed dates and places of birth. She made them show her what they would hand out if the Germans asked for their passports, and what they would produce if the French asked them if they possessed any foreign currency.

At last they were ready, and all they could do now was wait. Then one evening Anne received word that the two Americans were to leave at six o'clock on the following morning.

She awoke at 4.30 a.m. and made some coffee. Then she woke the two men and they started to dress.

Left Anne and Julien Brusselmans, seen here on the terrace of their home, helped set up the Comète line in 1940 and continued working for it until the Germans were driven out of Brussels. From his work-place on the ground floor of 127, Julien could telephone warnings of Gestapo activity.
Right The Brusselman's children Yvonne, aged 12, and Jacques, who was eight, helped protect escaping fliers—Jacques would run to close the door to delay unwelcome visitors.

The last lap

It was a little tricky for Anne to have to smuggle two men out of the house at this hour of the day. There were some nuns living in the next building, and they always went to mass just before six o'clock. Anne had to wait on the balcony until she had seen the nuns go off to mass before she could take the men down.

They said their 'good-byes' before they left the flat. Then she led the way to the elevator.

They were the only people in the street, and the clink of their footsteps seemed to fill it in the early morning air. As they hurried along, Anne had other things on her mind. Word had come through to expect three more Americans, one badly wounded, with a bullet in the leg. He would need bandages and ether, which were in very short supply. Getting them would involve seeking help from a chemist, who was not supposed to issue medicines without a prescription.

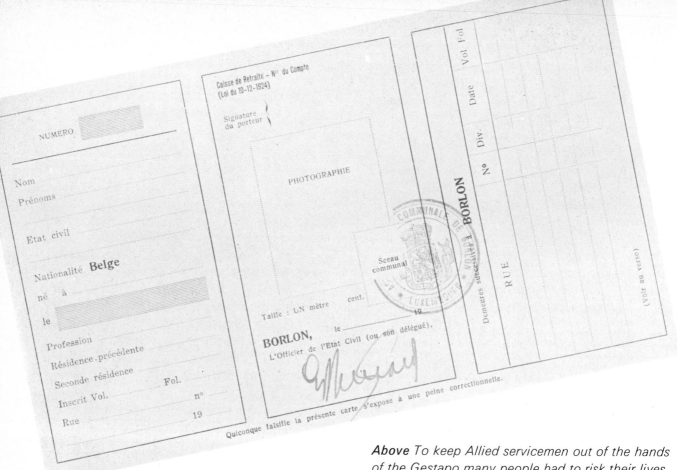

The two Americans, safely on their way to Paris with their new escorts, felt humble at the experience they had just been through, knowing that Anne Brusselmans and her family had risked their lives for them. Their peril was far greater than that of the airmen they helped, because if they were caught by the Gestapo they would be tortured and shot, whereas the airmen would merely become prisoners of war.

Above To keep Allied servicemen out of the hands of the Gestapo many people had to risk their lives to steal or make identity cards and movement permits, to fake official stamps, to forge official signatures and fill in personal details.
Right The Gestapo played rough. They would tear a suspect's apartment to pieces looking for links with an escape organization.

They reached the station. The streets outside were crowded with parked German command cars and covered troop trucks, and there were soldiers everywhere. SS men stood in groups at every entrance. They passed through into the wide main hall without a word. Anne recognized the French guide waiting casually by one of the notice boards as they passed him by. She turned abruptly to the two Americans and shook hands with them. Hank gave her a wink. She was gone, mingling with the crowd, heading for the exit.

The two Americans, safely on their way to Paris with their new escorts, felt humble at the experience they had just been through, knowing that Anne Brusselmans and her family had risked their lives for them. Their peril was far greater than that of the airmen they helped, because if they were caught by the Gestapo they would be tortured and shot, whereas the airmen would merely become prisoners of war.

They arrived safely back in England seven weeks later.

At that moment there were 49 Allied airmen hiding in Brussels. Their escape would be made possible by people from all walks of life —priests, nuns, doctors, nurses, shop-girls, factory workers, lawyers, engineers and members of the nobility. They gave unstinting help, including food, clothing and shelter, and, too often, their lives; and many an Allied airman, cocky and confident in his youth, learned humility in the presence of these people —people like Anne and Julien Brusselmans of 127 Rue d'Ixelles, Brussels —which came to be known as 'Rendezvous 127'.

After the war their services were recognized by honours from the Belgian, British and American governments.

THE WIRE-CUTTERS

Straight through the wire in broad daylight, that was American flier William Nicholls' plan for getting out of Stalag Luft III. But his theory that there was a blind spot required the cold-blooded nerve to cut a hole through the wire under the snouts of German-manned machine guns. Would it work?

Flying Officer William Nicholls (right) had been a Spitfire Pilot with the Eagle Squadron—a unit of American fliers that fought with the Royal Air Force. Their exploits verged on the legendary— flying at zero feet down a village street to drop bricks on German officers relaxing at cafe tables, landing under the protective wire strung across a strategic runway—and Nicholls carried the spirit into his escape. He and Flight-Lieutenant Ken Toft blitzed out straight through the barbed wire fence.

From the spring of 1942, when Goering's much vaunted **Stalag Luft III**, at Sagan, about 80 miles east of Berlin, was opened, Air Force prisoners began to be segregated from the Army; and whereas before, they had been housed largely in formidable moat-surrounded castles and hunting lodges such as Spangenberg, now the prisoners had to contend with barbed wire and a camp scientifically designed to prevent its inmates from getting out. Thus it was thought that once inside the stalag, the chances of a prisoner ever escaping were slim.

One day only a few weeks after the camp had opened, Flying Officer William Nicholls, an American who had been a Spitfire pilot with the famous Eagle Squadron which had fought as a unit of the RAF before the United States entered the war, was standing in the compound enjoying the sunshine and idly surveying the camp. He looked along the line of the three watch-towers on the eastern side of the perimeter. Being mathematically inclined, a thought struck him.

Wing Commander 'Wings' Day, Senior British Officer, at Stalag Luft III, helped plan many of the great escapes and stood guard for the wire-cutters.

The towers were just slightly out of line with the wire fence. From where the sentry stood, the angle of vision would be so oblique that towards the middle of the fence the posts would appear to close up, with nothing visible behind them. There must be a blind spot between the two guard posts, where a man lying on the ground would not be able to be seen by the guard in either tower.

Fascinated by the theory, he strolled along by the guard-rail, paused midway between the towers and looked across at the row of poles supporting the tangle of barbed wire. Maybe. It was just possible.

He thought about it for a few days, then quietly discussed it with Flight-Lieutenant Ken Toft—an RAF fighter pilot—who saw the validity of the theory at once.

A little later, they put their plan to the Escape Committee.

From then on, at a series of meetings, the pros and cons of their scheme were discussed. A night escape was ruled out at once. There had been several attempts in the past, and almost all of them had proved disastrous. The reason was simple. The barracks blocks were locked shortly after sunset, and anyone moving about the compound after dark could be spotted from the watch-towers. An escaper trying to cover the distance between the barracks and the wire fence made an easy target and was, in fact, asking to be shot.

And even if he succeeded in reaching the fence without being noticed, he had to then cut a hole through a complicated entanglement of barbed wire. There was no greater test of courage and endurance than to spend minutes cutting a tunnel through the wire and then to crawl out of the prison camp while it was being swept by searchlights and covered by machine-guns from the towers and from the German sentries who patrolled the outer perimeter.

In broad daylight

So a daylight escape it had to be—and on a fine day at that, when the prisoners would be out in the compound enjoying the sunshine and relaxing in various ways, reading or writing letters, or indulging in some sport, or simply strolling around the camp circuit just inside the guard-rail.

But some members of the Escape Committee were still unconvinced about the American's theory, even though he made a scale model and an accurate mechanical drawing and proved it mathematically. What was needed, they opined, was a chance to test the theory physically.

That summer, a new compound was being built on the northern side of the East Compound, and some of the prisoners were given the job of digging out tree stumps to clear space for a football ground.

One day, one of the prisoners got the opportunity of climbing up the ladder to one of

Above there were eight sentry towers at Stalag Luft III—this is the entrance to one—but there was still a blind spot at the base of the wire.

the watch-towers that had just been built. He looked along the row of fence posts which stood along the perimeter and knew at once that the American was right. From where he stood, the sentry would be unable to see a man lying on the ground midway between the towers.

There were some further talks with the Escape Committee, who decided that a diversion —or, better still, a number of diversions—would have to be arranged to distract the attention of the guards. This would give the escapers time to step over the guard-rail and walk across the ten yards of danger-zone to the wire fence and lie flat on the ground.

Another point: What about the guard at the gate? And the sentries in the outer towers? And the roving pickets patrolling outside the perimeter? Diversions appeared to be the answer. And timing.

And how would they dress? There would be no opportunity to change once they stepped outside the wire; and they couldn't very well appear in the compound after lunch wearing civilian clothes. The answer was that they would wear French khaki uniforms. Some of these had been issued to RAF personnel whose own uniforms had been torn or burned while they were baling out. Once outside the compound, they could pass themselves off as French prisoners who were working in the neighbour-

hood, and who frequently passed Stalag Luft III on their way to and from their own camp.

Gradually, the escape attempt took form, and no detail was left to chance. By now it was September, and all that was needed was a fine day.

The Squadron Leader checked his watch.

It was 1341 hours.

He went back to reading his paperback.

Sitting on a sawn-off tree-stump near the north-east corner of the compound, he looked a picture of serenity. It was a beautiful September day, and the prisoners in the East Compound of Stalag Luft III were scattered about the enclosure, immersed in a variety of activities that made the camp look like a holiday resort. Many were stripped to the waist to enjoy the last few days of the late-summer sun; some were idly kicking a football around the *appell* ground; down by the southern fence a small group was gathered around two boxers, whose seconds were tying on their respective fighter's gloves and offering advice; other prisoners strolled along

Stalag Luft III—this photograph shows the East and Centre compounds—was a hive of escape activity with tunnels driven from huts, attempts to smuggle prisoners out and breakouts over the wire all backed up with forgeries and disguises.

the path just inside the guard-rail. On the other side of the high barbed-wire fence a German sentry marched at a leisurely pace past the midway watch-tower and continued on toward the southern corner of the compound.

At 1343, Nicholls and Toft, wearing French uniforms sauntered from their hut to the northern fence, then strolled eastwards until they reached the corner, then turned southwards.

Looking like two close friends on an after-lunch stroll, they continued south just inside the guardrail.

The Squadron Leader had let his book drop from his hands and appeared to be dozing. At any rate, he was leaning back, his face tilted upwards to get more of the sun. His eyes were slits.

In the northern-most hut, a man was watching from one of the windows. Another man was standing like a statue by the door, as though waiting for a signal.

The two strollers reached a point midway between the two watch-towers. The Squadron Leader aroused himself, looked about him, then took out a white handkerchief and blew his nose.

The man at the window turned and said: 'Go!'

The man at the door turned and marched briskly on to the compound, heading directly toward the north-east tower.

At the instant there was a flurry of activity among the footballers, and suddenly their ball shot over the guard-rail just below the southern side of the midway watch-tower.

Coincidentally, this was also the moment that a prisoner who had been standing on his own by the gate at the northern end of the compound chose to start playing his accordion.

The man who had come from the hut had reached the foot of the north-east tower. He called up to the sentry, who leaned out of the box and asked what he wanted.

The prisoner asked him to telephone the Commandant at once and tell him that the Senior British Officer wanted to request an urgent interview. The sentry withdrew and picked up the telephone.

The men watching the boxing match were yelling their heads off as the two opponents slugged it out, an obvious grudge-match. One of the men knocked the other to the ground to the delight of the milling onlookers. The referee began counting.

A spokesman for the footballers was calling up to the sentry in the midway tower, asking if he might be given permission to step over the guard-rail to retrieve their football.

Danger zone

Meanwhile, half-way between the two eastern watch-towers, the two prisoners wearing French uniforms had nonchalantly stepped over the rail and walked across the ten yards of the 'danger zone' Now they lay flat on the ground at the base of the wire fence. And while the American kept watch, the Britisher began to cut a hole in the wire fence with a pair of home-made wire-cutters which he had slipped from under his tunic.

The German sentry continued at his leisurely pace towards the south-east corner of the compound.

A few yards away, the floored boxer struggled to his feet at the count of nine, urged on by his supporters, and the battle was on again amid the cheers of the men who formed the ring.

Up by the gate, the squeeze-box player was doing a jig to the tune of *There's a tavern in the town*.

The footballers had crowded by the guard rail to add their vocal support to their spokesman asking for permission to retrieve their football.

The prisoner at the foot of the north-east tower waited for word from the German Camp Commandant about the interview requested by the Senior British Officer.

And in the cook-house, one of the prisoner-cooks had accused the German NCO-in-charge of cutting down on rations, and a spirited argument was in progress.

Flight-Lieutenant Toft had succeeded in cutting a hole in the wire fence. He thrust his head and shoulders through it, then took from under his tunic some pointed sticks which he drove into the ground. Then he cut away the tangle of wire and twisted the strands around the sticks, making a narrow tunnel beneath the barricade. He wriggled along on his stomach as he cleared the way, and when he had cut away the final strands, passed the wire-cutters back to Nicholls, who threw them back to the guard-rail. One of the prisoners standing close by retrieved them

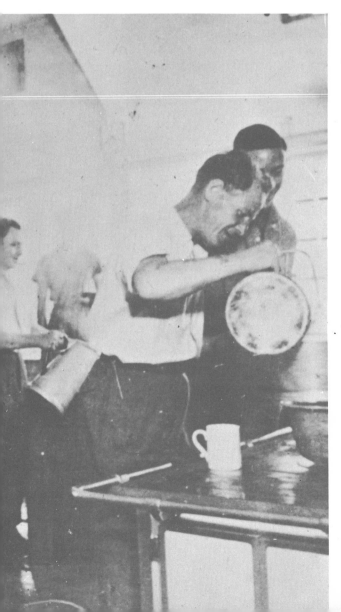

Every part of the camp could help in an escape attempt. The prisoner-cooks in the cook-house at Stalag Luft III **below** *staged a spirited argument with the German NCO to distract attention from Nicholls and Toft as they cut through the wire.*

and hid them under his tunic, then blew his nose loudly.

It was 1348 hours.

The spectators watching the boxing match roared their approval as the battle went on and the boxer who had survived the knock-out floored his opponent, causing the roving sentry to pause and watch the outcome.

The footballers had been given permission to retrieve their ball, and their spokesman slid across the guard rail and walked across the danger-zone under the watchful eye and the cocked gun of the guard in the tower.

The sentry in the north-east tower was annoyed with the prisoner standing below, who had just told him that the Senior British Officer had changed his mind and now didn't wish to see the Camp Commandant.

The accordion player was now playing *Lili Marlene*, to which the guard in the tower was listening appreciatively.

In the cook-house the German NCO had the floor and was proving beyond all doubt that he

Above Nicholls and Toft needed nine minutes to get clear. With over a thousand prisoners in the compound large-scale recreational activities could help confuse the guards.
Right For some prisoners a comfortable hut could become a home from home—but for escapers such as Nicholls it was just a place to plot.

was not short-rationing the prisoners, while the men stood around him listening dutifully.

We're through

Toft emerged from the wire tunnel, stood up quickly and dusted off the dirt from the front of his French uniform.

The American followed him through, wriggling forward under the wire. He reached the path outside the fence, stood up quickly and brushed himself down.

The two men walked leisurely southward as the roving picket came around the corner at the end of the compound and walked towards them.

The two 'Frenchmen' held their breath as the guard approached them. They plodded along, drew level, passed him by, continued on.

Would he notice the hole in the wire? They couldn't turn round to find out. As they passed the last tower the guard peered down at them. He looked about to speak, but changed his mind. He turned away to watch the boxing match. The two escapers went on. At the curve in the path, 75 yards further down, they disappeared into the woods.

Unaccountably, the roving sentry passed the hole in the barbed wire without noticing it.

The minutes passed. It was 1350—only nine minutes since the Squadron Leader had blown his nose.

Hundreds of men carried on with their allotted activities without ever once allowing their eyes to stray in the direction of the escaping prisoners. The camp slowly settled down. The boxing match came to a close, with both men still on their feet. The footballers resumed a desultory game. The musician wandered away from the gate, still playing.

Nothing happened for a further 15 minutes. Then, at 1415, it was time for the sentries in the towers to be changed. The relief guards came marching along outside the perimeter, and one by one each relief sentry went up and took over and the man on duty came down and joined the squad.

They reached the south-east guard-box, changed sentries, then marched northward. The midway tower; the change made smoothly; northward again.

A hundred pairs of eyes watched them surreptitiously as they approached the hole in the fence.

Suddenly the German NCO-in-charge halted

Room 5. Block 63. Stammlager Luft 3. July 12th 1942.

At the crucial moment, as Nicholls and Toft stepped into the danger zone, a group playing football kicked the ball beneath the midway watch tower—drawing the guard's attention.

in his tracks. He snapped an order and the men halted. Then he ran forward and looked at the hole. He produced a whistle and blew it shrilly.

The guard in the nearby watch-tower was on the phone, speaking quickly in German.

The alarm siren went off.

A minute later, a thousand prisoners in the compound watched anxiously as a squad of armed guards, with eager Alsatians straining at their leashes, set off down the path beyond the perimeter fence. The dogs bayed and whimpered as they passed the end of the camp. continued down the road for 70 yards, then swung off into the forest.

A long time later—more than three hours—they came back—without the two prisoners. The men in the compound cheered.

Nicholls and Toft were, in fact, safely away. By some miracle they had eluded the dogs. Two days later, at a point not 20 miles from the camp, they boarded a goods train heading west.

It was an unfortunate twist of fate that at that very moment the German SS in Berlin were engaged in a vigorous search for several Russian prisoners who had escaped from a nearby working party, and as Nicholls and Toft were nearing Berlin they were caught in the Gestapo's net. At first mistaken for Russians, they received harsh treatment at the hands of the Germans; but as soon as they were able to establish their identity they were returned to Stalag Luft III.

The camp authorities had already worked out how the escape had been managed and were building extensions to all watch-towers to eliminate blind spots and enable sentries to have a clear view of both sides of the barbed-wire barricade. This ensured that no similar attempt to escape was ever made.

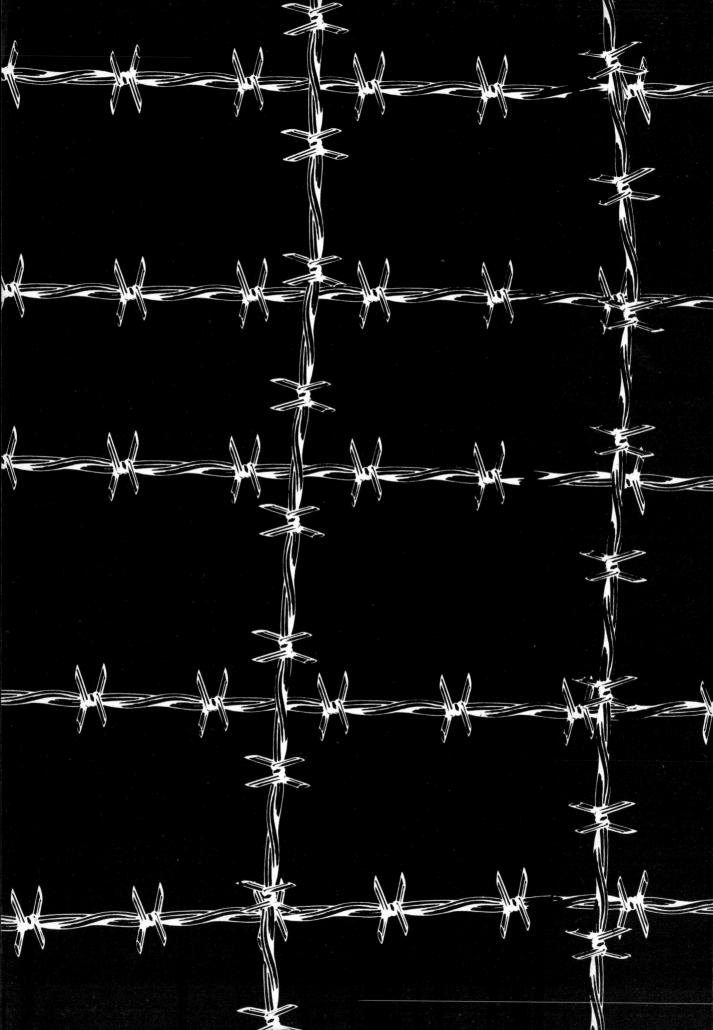